THE COMPLETE
CHEAPSKATE

THE COMPLETE
CHEAPSKATE

How to break free from money worries forever, without sacrificing your quality of life.

MARY HUNT

Publisher of *Cheapskate Monthly*

PUBLISHING
Colorado Springs, Colorado

THE COMPLETE CHEAPSKATE
Copyright © 1997 Mary Hunt
All rights reserved. International copyright secured.

Library of Congress Cataloging-in-Publication Data
Hunt, Mary, 1948–
    The complete cheapskate / Mary Hunt
        p. cm.
    ISBN 1-56179-520-8
    1. Finance, Personal—Unites States.   2. Finance, Personal—Planning.
3. Saving and thrift—United States.   I. Title.
    HG179.H8548 1997
    332.024—dc21   96-39785
                                                               CIP

Published by Focus on the Family Publishing, Colorado Springs, Colorado 80995.
Distributed in the U.S.A. and Canada by Word Books, Dallas, Texas.

Focus on the Family books are available at special quantity discounts when purchased in bulk by corporations, organizations, churches, or groups. Special imprints, messages, and excerpts can be produced to meet your needs. For more information, write: Special Sales, Focus on the Family Publishing, 8605 Explorer Drive, Colorado Springs, CO 80920, or call (719) 531-3400 and ask for the Special Sales Department.

All Scripture references are taken from the HOLY BIBLE, NEW INTERNATIONAL VERSION ® (NIV) ®. Copyright © 1973, 1978, 1984 by International Bible Society. Used by permission of Zondervan Publishing House. All rights reserved.

Portions of this book were originally published under the titles *The Best of the Cheapskate Monthly* and *The Cheapskate Monthly Money Makeover,* both by St. Martin's Press.

Articles in Appendix A and tips in Appendix B are reprinted with permission of *Cheapskate Monthly.* Copyright © 1992-1996, *Cheapskate Monthly*, P.O. Box 2135, Paramount, CA 90723-8135; (310) 630-6474.

Editor: Keith Wall
Cover Design: BC Studios

Printed in the United States of America
97 98 99 00/10 9 8 7 6 5 4 3 2 1

This book is lovingly dedicated to the thousands of people who make up the *Cheapskate Monthly* family. You have encouraged me with your loyalty, strength, and determination. I consider it a privilege to walk beside you on the path of financial solvency.

Contents

Acknowledgments

I wish to thank the thousands of people who have written to me over the past five years. Your candor, courage, and progress reports have encouraged me more than you will ever know. Your enthusiasm and approval rates have annihilated my perceived personal limitations, and your willingness to share your personal financial struggles and remarkable progress have contributed to the success of *Cheapskate Monthly.*

Special thanks to my assistant Cathy Hollenbeck for her constant help, invaluable expertise, and loyal support; and to Keith Wall and the wonderful folks at Focus on the Family Publishing for caring enough to make this book available to the Christian market.

Special thanks to my wonderful husband, Harold, and sons, Jeremy and Josh, for their love and patience and for never complaining when the table is covered with books and manuscripts instead of dinner. I love you.

Who Are You Calling a Cheapskate?!

I am certain that many of you are completely turned off by the term *cheapskate*. At first, I was, too. But please hear me out. I had to come up with a term that implies the complete opposite of a spendthrift, and I think *cheapskate* fits the bill. Give it time—it will grow on you.

Let me explain what I mean by a *cheapskate*, and I think you'll agree it's a positive label. A cheapskate:

- Does not spend more money than he/she earns, no matter how desperate or tempting the situation might appear.

- Has a spirit of generosity, regularly sharing money, time, and other resources with people in need.

- Lives honestly and ethically, regardless of the temptation to do otherwise in order to get a better deal.

- Saves at least 10 percent of all income.

- Does not buy compulsively but makes intelligent and well-thought-out choices.

- Lives within a financial plan that includes a margin to allow for fun and spontaneity.

That's it! Nothing negative or shameful. Being a cheapskate is honorable. You see, there is absolutely nothing wrong with having nice things or having dreams and goals for achievement and success. But we get into trouble when we demand the right to have things *now* by diving head-over-heels into debt through the improper use of credit. We also create problems for ourselves when we allow money and material possessions to dominate our thoughts and motivations.

A cheapskate, as I define it, is one who has a balanced, honest, and dignified approach to money management.

Something else you must understand: There are two types of cheapskates. First, there is the natural-born kind. This is a person who is naturally thrifty and probably never bounced a check, made a compulsive purchase, or took on debt. I am in awe of you natural-borns, and please let the rest of us learn from you.

Second, there are the converted cheapskates. This is the category into which I—and most people—fall. Even though I was born into a thrifty family and I grew up observing and living a frugal lifestyle, it did not "stick." I must have been a natural-born spendthrift. But I am a living example that conversion is possible.

Cheapskates also have many different approaches. I do not personally advocate a "bag lady" style. I don't collect cans along the beach or go through industrial trash bins. But you should see me stretch a dollar at the grocery store. I don't cram my philosophy down anyone's throat, and I don't impose my personal style on family or friends. I like to think that I am a classy, dignified cheapskate. For example, I would prefer one very nice outfit rather than 10 from the thrift store. I would live frugally 50 weeks of the year to allow for a nice family vacation. I am more interested in finding new ways to save cash, cut medical/auto insurance costs, open my own money market account with $100, or learning how to keep my car in good repair for the least amount of money rather than saving egg cartons with the hopes of thinking up some meaningful use! The thought of buying a piece of income-producing property is far more exciting to me than recycling aluminum foil. But that's just me. Others have a different philosophy, and that's fine.

I am proud to be a cheapskate, and I'm excited to share this way of life with you. By the time you finish this book, you, too, will be proud to be called a cheapskate.

Chapter 1

....

Been There, Done That: My Story

*How I Went From Spendthrift
to Cheapskate*

I used to be anything but a cheapskate. I broke into a cold sweat at even
the thought of being considered cheap. And I was driven to make
absolutely sure a clear line of demarcation was drawn between me in
my world and those pitiful souls residing in the land of Cheap. I charged
my way through life feeling quite entitled because I had every credit card
known to the English-speaking world.

It all started quite innocently with a promise. As a child, I was a
daydreamer, a future-planner. I grew up embarrassed that I had to wear

5

hand-me-down clothes and things purchased at the secondhand store. I, the Scarlett O'Hara of the '50s, vowed that I would never be poor and that my children would never wear clothes from the thrift shop. Just like waving a magic wand, I guaranteed my adult status and that of my children. If only I had been wise enough to make a similar vow regarding a way to pull it off.

Within days of my wedding, I cautiously suggested to my new husband, Harold, that we should look into getting a gasoline credit card. After all, now that we were married, we were entering a new social stratum, and every real family must be prepared for unforeseen emergencies. We needed to get with the program and stop depending on cash so much. We needed plastic! Harold went along with the idea, and before I knew it we received two shiny new credit cards, one bearing my name. Wow! "Free" gas whenever I wanted! No longer would I have to dig around for loose change in order to pump a few gallons into my car. I could fill up whenever the mood struck, and I knew that never again would I be concerned with mundane issues such as the price of gas. It felt good to carry clout. Being a married woman was quite prestigious.

It seemed only logical that we should have an alternative brand of gas available (just in case we were away from our regular station), so we applied for a second set of credit cards. After all, if one was good, two would be better. Those came more quickly and with less effort than the first. I could feel our status soaring to new heights, and I carried the proper credentials to prove it.

By the time our babies came along, the first credit card had been canceled by the gasoline company. We'd been late with some monthly payments and missed a few altogether. Now who would have thought a big company with all that money would demand that we pay it back, in full, every month? Not to worry, though. In addition to an assortment of gasoline cards, I'd added every department store card in Southern California.

It was so easy. If a particular store didn't automatically send me preapproved cards in the mail, all I had to do was pick up an application in the store. It became a game somewhat like collecting baseball cards. I was compelled to acquire credit cards—they gave me a sense of freedom and status. You must understand that I didn't apply for the cards with a specific purchase in mind; rather, I wanted the security I believed they would bring us. I rationalized that we needed them in case of emergencies. Little did I know that the very things I thought would provide security were to become a catalyst for crisis.

Harold was soon promoted to middle management in a large, prestigious California bank. I couldn't have been more proud. One of the perks of his benefits package was an unsolicited bank card—with a very handy line of credit. Now, not only was I "entitled" to all the gas I could use, the department store cards and bank card prepared me for any kind of unforeseen emergency. And unlike the gasoline companies, the others didn't require full payment each month. The companies were quite pleased to allow a small monthly payment. What's more, the companies all but pronounced a blessing over me every time I used them.

Soon I found my life filled with many little "emergencies." Often they were manufactured from my poring over department store catalogs that showed up in the mail. My overactive mind and impulsive tendencies would join forces to convince me of an urgent need. I would become privately fixated on a certain item and be unable to relax until I found a way to get it. I felt a certain, albeit temporary, high when I bought the latest in kids' clothing or GI Joe action figures for my boys. I felt justified in spending huge sums in fabric stores. I would buy everything needed for project after project, telling myself I could make all kinds of clothes and decorator items for far less than the store-bought equivalents. In reality, I completed few of the projects, and the materials became piles in the garage, destined to be included in the next Goodwill donation.

One of the best parts of being a cardholder was this: The more I used those credit cards and continued making the minimum monthly payments, the better standing and status the card companies bestowed on me. Why else would they keep increasing my limits? When the bank credit card limit reached the four-figure mark, I just knew they thought I was fantastic. And

I was certainly keeping the promise I'd made to myself: I was not poor, and my kids did not wear clothes from the thrift store. We certainly *looked* good.

Shopping became even easier in the seclusion and comfort of my home. With a phone in one hand and a mail-order catalog in the other, I could create the windfall of Christmas for myself and my children any time I had a whim. I realize now I was attempting to go back and fix my own childhood by giving my children all the clothes, toys, and attention I had missed. I was trying to fill a void by giving gifts that were bigger and better than the recipient could believe. I was making up for what I'd lacked, fulfilling my vow that my kids and I would never be poor and that I would always have the approval and the acceptance of my friends—even if I had to buy both. I lived out the only agenda I knew: External appearances are all-important. Anything going on inside that conflicts with a perfect facade must be ignored, denied, and put aside.

My instruments of entitlement were not limited only to credit cards. I had a checkbook. While I considered credit card spending to be long-term deferment (like hundreds of years from now), writing checks was short-term deferment. Often I neglected to record the checks I wrote. It was safer that way because Harold couldn't track my spending. His tendency to be unobservant became my ally. I could all but redecorate the entire house and he wouldn't notice.

I worked under the philosophy that somehow by the time the check was ready to clear, I would magically come up with funds I could sneak into the bank account. Of course, it rarely happened, but I still wrote checks, often with reckless abandon. One of two things happened over and over again. I either overdrew the account or brought the balance down so low that when Harold went to pay bills, there was no longer enough to get us through the month.

Writing rubber checks was bad enough, but to make matters worse, Harold was the bank manager! Let me assure you that such behavior from employees is not looked upon kindly by your average financial institution. Imagine his embarrassment and rage when one of his staff members sheepishly advised him of the situation and suggested that he make an immediate deposit. The phone calls I received when that happened are memories I'd rather forget. And you think *your* blood runs cold when the bank calls!

More than once, my actions placed Harold's job in jeopardy, but I still couldn't stop my outrageous behavior. I was not making enormous purchases—certainly not new cars or expensive jewelry. I was five-and-ten-dollaring us to death.

Inwardly, I felt frail, weak, and insignificant. The act of spending gave me momentary sensations of power and strength. I temporarily felt cared for and nurtured. Those were wonderful feelings, and I made sure I experienced them often.

As time went on, things got pretty sticky, especially around the first of each month. I had incurred such heavy consumer debt (all those credit accounts accruing interest at rates of 18 percent and up) that our monthly expenses exceeded our income. Fortunately for us—or so I thought—we were benefiting greatly from the real estate boom of the '70s and '80s. Each time we got too far behind, we refinanced the house, pulling out our precious equity and plunging ourselves deeper and deeper into trouble. And of course, the higher mortgage payments eventually put us right back where we'd been. We bought into the debt consolidation theory: Take out one big loan to pay off all the small ones and end up with a more manageable payment each month. What a terrible mistake that was! Slowly but surely, the accounts paid off with the consolidation loan proceeds inched their way back up to the limit, and we were in worse shape than ever.

I was convinced that Harold's work in banking would never provide the level of income I felt necessary to live the lifestyle we'd chosen and that he needed to look at other career options—ones where big bucks would be available. So when an opportunity came along to try self-employment, he said good-bye to the bank, 16 years of tenure, and regular paychecks. We took another financial plunge.

Together we made some crucial blunders. We were driven by the fantasy of getting rich quick, and we went blindly into a multi-level

marketing and sales business that we knew nothing about. Worse, we did
it with borrowed funds. It's no wonder that in only four months, our first
entrepreneurial endeavor ended in an abrupt and devastating failure . . .
and the loss of all the money we'd borrowed.

Our debts were enormous, our income nonexistent. Now both Harold
and I were unemployed, and the anxiety and turmoil became unbearable.
Seeing no way out of the mess, I became terrified and desperate. I'd run
out of options and clever schemes to deal with emergencies. I felt like a
magician with amnesia, a plate spinner with paralysis, a juggler who'd just
had her arms amputated. I'd brought together all the elements that
frequently prompt a divorce, bankruptcy, the loss of the home, and the
destruction of the family. I felt that everything in my life was on the verge
of meltdown. It was only when I hit absolute rock bottom that I was willing to consider change, no matter how radical. Finally, I'd come to the
place where I was willing to do anything to alleviate the most horrible pain
I'd ever known.

I vividly recall that Saturday afternoon in 1982—the day I finally faced
reality. I needed to get away by myself to think things through, and I
ended up at my in-laws' house. More than likely, I was looking for the
kind of comfort and reassurance only parents know how to give, but that
particular day, no one was home. Looking back, I see clearly that God
needed to take me to His woodshed, to teach me a hard lesson. What I
needed was the truth—however painful—and not soothing words from
parents telling me that everything would be okay.

There's never been a time before or since that I can remember feeling
so hopeless. Sure, my faith in God was real. I'd accepted Jesus Christ as my
Savior when I was young. But I'd never depended on God when it came
to finances. I'd never allowed God's power to invade my life. I trusted in
my credit cards and my own schemes more than God's promises. That
day, as I sat in the silence and emptiness of my in-laws' house, it was as if
God turned on the floodlights of heaven to illuminate the dark caverns of
my life. For the first time I saw in living color the magnitude of the mess
I'd made. I'd been deceptive, deceitful, and manipulative. I'd lied and

cheated in order to have things my way. And I was certain that I'd all but destroyed my husband's life.

As I began to deal honestly with my situation, I asked for God's forgiveness and help to rebuild my life. As I prayed and poured out my problems and worries to God, I was comforted by Scripture verses that came to mind:

How can You ever forgive me?

"If we confess our sins, he is faithful and just and will forgive us our sins and purify us from all unrighteousness" (1 John 1:9).

How can I go on?

"My grace is sufficient for you, for my power is made perfect in weakness" (2 Corinthians 12:9).

I've done such horrible things. I'm consumed by shame. What should I do?

"He who ignores discipline comes to poverty and shame, but whoever heeds correction is honored" (Proverbs 13:18).

Please let me keep my husband, children, and home.

"Delight yourself in the LORD and he will give you the desires of your heart" (Psalm 37:4).

There in the kitchen, I fell to my knees and begged God's forgiveness for the horrible mess I'd created. I made a new promise: I would stop my irrational spending and debting, and I would do whatever it took to pay back whatever we owed. I asked God to help me change. I realized that I had far more control over my spending than I had ever wanted to admit. I no longer had to convince anyone, including myself, that I wasn't poor.

I understood something else—though both Harold and I had made big mistakes, it was primarily *me* who had brought us to the point of financial (and emotional) ruin. I needed to start making major financial contributions to our marriage partnership. I had made far too many withdrawals. Willing to do anything (fear is a great motivator), I accepted a full-time job that was offered to me about 10 days later. Because I had earned my real estate license, I was able to combine property management with sales, providing a steady income plus commissions. It was a good thing, too, because Harold decided he needed to stay home for a while. I became the breadwinner.

What a turn of events! We immediately eliminated all day-care costs. Two little boys got to spend huge amounts of time with their dad, and I was relieved of the pressure that many working moms experience because Harold took over the household tasks. We switched roles, and it was awkward at first. But I adapted quickly. Being scared witless was probably the best thing that could have happened to me.

At the same time, we had to learn frugality—a new concept. It didn't come naturally by any means. But we were shocked at how much we were able to cut back. The most amazing thing, though, is that no one, including the kids, really noticed our scaled-back standard of living. It just goes to show that others are not nearly as impressed with our artificial lifestyles as we think they should be.

Gradually, as we were able to reverse our spending habits, we began to get out of debt, and our drastically reduced living requirements became our way of life. Things went so well that in 1985 we were able to go into business for ourselves in a more practical and sensible way. With backgrounds in banking and real estate, we opened our own industrial real estate company.

If all of this sounds too easy, understand that I'm telling the condensed version of our story. Nothing happened overnight. In fact, it took the next 13 years to get completely out of debt. While we did pay back every single dime of interest, penalties, and principal, the scars will be with us forever. We will always wonder what might have been had I not been so financially foolish. But one step at a time, we continue to make progress. And I am still learning that my dignity and self-worth do not come from possessions and I cannot be dependent on the number of credit cards I carry.

Thankfully, we didn't have to file for bankruptcy, we didn't lose the house, and best of all, our marriage has been strengthened by the tremendous challenges we've faced. We learned to save money and our two sons have grown into fine young men who have learned financial responsibility right alongside us.

After struggling for 10 years not only to make ends meet every month but also to make significant repayments toward the massive debts I had run up, in October 1991 I became impatient with the snail's pace the process was taking. My impatience drove me to think of some way I could increase our income in order to get this repayment thing over and done with. And quickly! We had better things to work for, and quite frankly, I was tired of living with monthly reminders of the pathetic mistakes I'd made.

Trying my hand at writing a newsletter seemed like a good idea. I certainly had a timely topic, lots of material, and lessons from the school of hard knocks. Since I already had an office established, I was pretty much set up to start another business. The writing part was an unknown, but I felt confident enough to at least give it a shot. Having mastered the effective business letter, I figured a newsletter would have some of the same characteristics.

So on January 1, 1992, *Cheapskate Monthly* premiered. It received a surprisingly positive response from readers across the U.S. and Canada. Today, more and more subscribers are requesting the newsletter, and they're learning that with a little ingenuity, perseverance, and determination, it is possible to live within your means without sacrificing your dignity or quality of life.

God has taken the mistakes and blunders in my life and begun to weave a tapestry of unbelievable beauty. I cannot express how thankful I am.

Cheapskate? Who me? You bet!

Are You a Good Money Makeover Candidate?

*Diligence, Not Miracles,
Brings Results*

M akeovers. Wonderful, aren't they? Someone waves a magic wand
and—*poof!*—everything that was unattractive is miraculously new
and remarkably gorgeous.

My favorite makeovers are the ones featured on television shows,
because I don't have to wait for the results. Through the miracle of TV, I
get to see the pathetic "before" at the beginning of the show and the sensa-
tional "after" at the end. I do exactly what the show producers hope I will:
I watch the entire show just to see the makeover result.

Call me overly sentimental, but I actually cried when an unsuspecting lady of the house opened the door of her home, revealing a complete decorating makeover compliments of daytime TV's most popular talk show. She cried and I cried along with her (mostly out of jealousy, I'm sure). They spent big bucks to make sure it was a successful show, and the ploy worked.

Makeover. It's an amazing word that says, "You aren't looking that great. You could use some improvement. You need help. I can fix you." Makes you wonder how those people in the magazines and on the TV shows feel when they receive the phone call offering them a makeover. Or how about the homes, faces, or bodies the editors and producers consider and then pass over? How would you like to be considered for a makeover and then rejected for lack of potential? That could require some serious time on the therapist's couch.

But not every face or every home needs a makeover. Imagine the lunacy of a popular magazine offering to do a makeover on Cindy Crawford or a home improvement show calling the White House to offer its services.

There's one kind of makeover, however, that most people could benefit from—a Money Makeover. How about you? Are you a hopeless case, or are you in such good shape that a Money Makeover would not only be useless, but an insult to your fine money management skills? If you are experiencing joy and an absence of stress, if the few bills that you do have are paid on time, if you are not rolling over debt from one month to the next, and if you feel well prepared for the future, congratulations! You really don't need a Money Makeover. In fact, you should get in that other line with Cindy Crawford.

But the fact that you picked up this book leads me to believe that you might welcome improvement. Perhaps you need only a minor adjustment to get yourself back on track. Or maybe you have been derailed and require more intensive work to get yourself rolling again.

Basically, there are only two requirements to qualify for a Money Makeover—desire and capacity. If you are ready to take back control of your finances, relieve the stress money has created, and prepare for the future, then you are more than qualified in the desire category. If you earn money (no matter how much or how little) and are obligated to pay bills, you also have the capacity.

Situations That Call for Action

Following are some real and recurring financial situations. See if any of these scenarios sound familiar to you.

Situation #1: You get an income tax refund because you generously overpaid the government last year, asking the IRS to keep what it needs and send you the balance sometime after April 15—without interest, of course. Since you can't decide whether to put the money toward an outstanding debt or replace your beyond-repair washing machine, you "wisely" put the money into your checking account so you won't be tempted to spend it. A month or so later, you decide the washing machine replacement idea has moved from optional to obligatory. You check your current checking account balance and are flabbergasted when you realize that the money is gone! (This prompts a few cross words with your spouse, since this kind of thing is always the *other person's* fault.) Somehow the entire tax refund has been absorbed into your everyday living expenses. Since you *need* a washing machine and you no longer have the cash that would have allowed you to consider a good used machine, you reluctantly go ahead and purchase a new one on credit.

Situation #2: Things have been going well for a while, and for the first time in a long time you actually have a few bucks left at the end of the month. You decide to go ahead and get the new patio furniture you've been eyeing. No sooner is the beautiful set delivered than your car breaks down. There's no way you could have predicted this. And the prognosis is not good. You need major repairs that are going to cost more than $600. Just what you need! Another crisis. Since you have no excess cash in the old checking account and no savings, you have no choice but to go to the bank and take a cash advance on your credit card. This emergency is so dire that you don't even worry about the interest rate.

Situation #3: You've been planning a family vacation. You really need to get away, and the kids are excited. You've been meaning to start saving for the trip, but something seems to come up every month. Before you know it, it's time to make the reservations, and you don't have a dime set aside for the vacation. You rationalize that family time is a priority, that this trip is a once-in-a-lifetime opportunity, and besides, you work hard and you deserve a vacation just like all of your friends and coworkers. Now is certainly not the time to worry about the cost of things. You want to show the family a good time. You decide to put the trip on your credit card but promise yourself you'll make huge payments when you get home to pay it off quickly. (How many times have you said that before?)

Situation #4: You've lived in your house for seven years (could it possibly be that long?), and you still don't have living room furniture. The master bedroom looks the same as it did the day you moved in and will look gorgeous as soon as you get a little extra cash to decorate. You have plans. You know exactly how you want to decorate and furnish those rooms . . . just as soon as you get some extra money. Weeks, months, and years keep flying by and still no extra money. You are embarrassed about how the place looks, so you find yourself avoiding guests. Every time you visit a friend's home, you feel pitiful and envious and leave feeling unhappy about your own house.

Situation #5: You carry a $250 deductible on your auto insurance in order to get the lower semiannual premiums. Wouldn't you know it? The one and only time you forget to look behind you before backing out of the grocery store parking lot, you smack into a stupid little pole. You hit it so hard that you ram the rear fender right into the rear wheel. Total repairs: $1,200! You just don't have an extra $250 for the deductible, but your car is not drivable. What choice do you have? Your credit cards are all maxed out. Financial disasters don't often give a warning, so how in the world were you supposed to plan ahead? You are forced to go to your parents. They reluctantly spring for the cash, but you know what's going to happen. You are surely in for another lecture, and until you pay them back, you are going to feel guilty. The last time you borrowed from them, they made you feel like a little kid again. You just hate doing this, but what alternatives do you have? You can't live without a car.

Situation #6: You just moved into a new apartment, one with lots of windows and daylight. You are thoroughly ashamed of your living room furniture, which you realized was a bit tired in the old place but has suddenly dropped to horrible in its new surroundings. You happen to read an ad in the newspaper announcing a going-out-of-business furniture sale. You drop in just to see what they have and drop out an hour later with a nifty easy-payment contract in your pocket. You are tickled with how easily you were able to arrange financing on an eight-piece collection with classic French styling in the tradition of master European craftsmen. Who cares what the financing charges are? You were able to pull off the deal with no money down!

Situation #7: You have a secret that is eating you alive. You have run up nearly $12,000 in credit card debt during the last year alone, and your wife has absolutely no idea. You handle the family finances, and while it's been tough, you've been able to juggle pretty well to keep her from finding out. When you took a slight pay cut last year, getting a few new preapproved credit cards seemed like a prudent thing to do—just in case. You didn't mention them to your wife because you knew she would just worry more about the money situation, and she depends so much on your ability to handle the finances. You didn't intend to start using the cards, but they seemed so available and with the household funds being so tight temporarily (the company promised to restore your pay rate as soon as possible), paying for things with the cards did seem like the best way.

A year later your salary has not increased, but your debt sure has. You've arranged to have the bills sent to the office, and creditors are starting to call you at work because you just can't keep up with those payments. You're scared to death that your wife or boss will find out. The only way out is to apply for more loans just to keep the minimum monthly payments current.

If you identified with any of these situations, you will definitely benefit from a Money Makeover. I want to show you how to handle your money so that these situations (which happen to everyone) won't disrupt your life. I want to teach you how to prepare for them, how to rework your finances so that you can relax and enjoy life. I'm even going to convince you to get out of debt. And I'm going to show you how to do it quickly—not the so-slowly-that-you-will-pay-lots-of-interest way your creditors have in mind.

Still not convinced that a Money Makeover should be in your future? Grab a pencil and take the following mini-quiz. Simply answer yes or no:

1. I spend much of my take-home income paying credit card bills.
2. I am near, at, or over the limit on my lines of credit.
3. I am regularly late paying my bills.
4. I often must pay late penalties.
5. I make only the minimum payment on my charge account.
6. I have to pay half my bills one month and half the next month because I can't pay all of them at the same time.
7. I write postdated checks.
8. I've bounced three checks in the last year.
9. I often "overshop" to meet the minimum-purchase requirement for credit card transactions.
10. I've taken a cash advance on one credit card to make the payment on another card.
11. I have to work overtime just to meet my current financial obligations.
12. I don't know exactly how much I owe in installment debts.
13. I worry about money quite a bit.
14. I do not have a regular savings program.
15. I carry a balance from month to month on at least one credit card and keep hoping to pay it off completely.
16. Some months I do pretty well, but other months I'm caught off guard by unexpected expenses.

17. I live from paycheck to paycheck and would be in big trouble if I lost my job.
18. I'd love to make charitable contributions, but it's impossible. There's just not enough money to go around. I *am* my own favorite charity.
19. I believe that if I made more money, I'd be just fine.
20. Creditors are calling all the time, and I just don't know how long I'll be able to juggle everything.
21. I use credit cards to buy things I would never purchase with cash.
22. I have applied for more than five credit cards in the past year.
23. I regularly pay for groceries with a credit card because I just don't have the cash.
24. My credit cards make me feel secure. There's a sense of freedom that comes with the ability to charge things.
25. I have lied to my spouse or creditors about making payments.

If you answered no to all of the foregoing, you obviously know how to control your spending and manage your resources in an intelligent and reasonable manner. If you answered yes to three or fewer statements, you are probably okay for now, but you should consider this a warning sign. Unless you change your ways, problems do lie ahead for you. A Money Makeover is probably the very best thing you could do to stop heading downhill.

If you answered yes to four or more statements, stick with me, kid. Keep reading this book, and you'll learn how to get out of this mess.

You're Not Alone

To reassure you that you are not alone, let me share some of the information I have gleaned from researching money matters and corresponding with the thousands of people who have written to me in the past several years. Ninety percent of your friends and relatives know very little about money management. Eighty percent of all Americans have never had a savings account, and only 10 percent of the total population have any idea how to control their spending.

There are approximately 1 *billion* active credit cards in this country as of this writing. Statistics indicate that only 28 percent of these cardholders pay their balances in full every 30 days. That means 720 million credit card accounts carry balances month after month, year after year. This represents millions of people who are hopelessly doomed to live their lives imprisoned by perma-debt. (Perma-debt is that dreadful condition brought about by revolving debt, which rolls over from month to month, year to year, decade to decade, following its victim right to the grave.)

So why do so few people actually do something about their financial woes? Partly because a major characteristic of human nature is laziness. Many people are looking for a no-effort way to make their lives perfect. They want someone to fix their problems. Believe it or not, I've found that a great majority of people in the worst financial trouble are willing to remain miserable until they win the lottery or are surprised by a big inheritance. While waiting, they continue to live in misery, limping through life, complaining all the way.

Many Americans have gotten into the bad habit of demanding "it" now and paying for "it" later. We have learned to feel entitled, and we think nothing of accepting 36 easy payments and a myriad of other marketing ploys. I hope that before too many more pages into this book, you will be convinced that living this way is not going to do anything but keep you headed in a downward spiral, a killer spiral of uncontrollable debt and bondage.

Many people sincerely want to do something about their out-of-control financial situations but don't know how. Where do they go to find practical, affordable, and effective help? For those in major crises, there are 12-step programs, credit counseling organizations, and bankruptcy protection. But most people have not reached the point of requiring such intensive and dramatic intervention. A reasonable alternative is a Money Makeover.

If you are lazy and have no intention of working at your own makeover, you will not be successful because I promise you no miracles, no magic. But I can promise that if you carefully follow this plan, you will experience remarkable results. You know how lousy your "before" picture looks. Just wait to see how good your "after" picture will be!

Chapter 3

Developing Healthy Money Attitudes

*Progress Begins with Transforming
Your Heart and Mind*

Regardless of your present financial situation, and regardless of the subtle or subconscious roles money has played in your life, you are not destined to live one more day under the control of your current money attitudes. The way that you have handled your money up to this point is probably the result of learned behaviors. I don't know about you, but I received absolutely no education on the simple matter of money and its role in my life, so it's no wonder I just played it by ear and did what came naturally.

Now you have a choice. Either you can continue with the bad habits that have landed you in need of a Money Makeover, or you can replace them with new, effective, and far more appropriate attitudes. In fact, developing healthy attitudes toward money is the first step to finding financial freedom and peace of mind. You can learn all the money-saving strategies and budgeting principles, but if you don't transform the underlying beliefs and perspectives that drive harmful financial practices, you won't make any *lasting* changes.

Let me make this perfectly clear: No matter how much you feel dominated by money, no matter how addicted you think you are to using your credit cards and to overspending, you have the ability to stop this outrageous behavior. You are not powerless over money's force in your life. You have the ability to make choices and control your actions. And you can change your actions anytime you set your mind to it. By repeating a new action over and over again, you will change your attitudes. And when your attitudes change, your behavior changes, and the new action becomes automatic. Researchers tell us that it takes three weeks—just 21 days—to create a new habit, and another three weeks to establish it for a lifetime.

As your attitudes about money change, something remarkable will happen. You will learn what truly constitutes abundance, and you will come to enjoy financial ease—not necessarily wealth, but contentment and a sense of well-being. You will see the focus of your life change from financial chaos to serenity and fulfillment.

Following are 10 healthy attitudes about money. I have written them in the first person so that as you read them, they will immediately become personal.

New Attitude #1: I choose to understand the truth about money.

I know that money cannot be equated with love, happiness, worth, respect, social standing, approval, acceptance, or goodness, nor can it purchase any of these things for me.

Money is simply a valuable commodity with which I am compensated for the use of my abilities, skills, and talents. Money is a convenient form of exchange for goods and services. It provides a means to a worthy end for me and my family. I can abuse money, or I can put it to good use. I acknowledge that as money flows into my life, my responsibility will increase, because to whom much is given, much is required.

Now that I've got it through my thick head exactly what money can and cannot do, I am free to find genuine and lasting sources of happiness, joy, approval, peace, and goodness. Wow, what a feeling!

New Attitude #2: I commit to being responsible and honest.

I acknowledge that it is irresponsible to write checks before the funds are in my account, make purchases on credit when I know I don't have the resources to repay the debt immediately, fail to balance my checking account, not work up to my abilities, and put off paying my bills. I further acknowledge that it is dishonest to mislead my creditors, fail to pay my taxes, hide my purchases, and conceal my debts from my spouse. I commit to a new way of life, one of total integrity in which I refuse to spend more money than I have. Now I will respond openly and honestly in all of my financial affairs.

New Attitude #3: I will not spend money that is not mine.

I commit to incur no more unsecured debt (credit cards, personal loans, and so on). I won't borrow from a friend, accept a service that I will pay for later, take a loan from a bank, charge anything on any credit card that cannot be repaid immediately, or in any way pledge future income for present goods and services. No one can force me to go into debt one more cent.

New Attitude #4: I will respond appropriately.

In the past I have used money inappropriately to make myself feel good, reverse bad moods, kill the pain of disappointment, make up for losses, feed my empty heart, fill my loneliness, anesthetize my sadness, and try to gain love and approval. Not only have I failed to deal with the real issues in my life, I have ended up with a pile of debts.

From now on when I encounter discouragement, stress, disappointment, or loneliness, I will not spend money in an effort to avoid facing the real, underlying problem. Instead I will face the situation head-on and deal with the issues in a healthy way, which will cause me to grow and will not put my solvency at risk.

New Attitude #5: I accept the responsibility and reject the shame.

I acknowledge that I am responsible for my present financial situation. I have made some mistakes. I have failed to plan ahead appropriately. But I am not the sum of my debts; my bank balance does not define who I am, and my creditors do not own me. I owe them money, which I will repay, but I do not owe them my life. No matter how painful or troubled my past has been, it is my *past*. I am now facing the future joyfully and hopefully, and I am looking forward to solvency.

New Attitude #6: I commit to clarity.

I acknowledge that because I have no idea where my money goes, I have allowed it to disappear. As part of my process toward solvency, I commit to record the simple *details* of how I spend my money. I commit to face the truth on a daily basis by keeping my purchases recorded, my checkbook balanced, my mail opened, and my bills in order and paid on time.

New Attitude #7: I will exercise my dreams.

This is my life. It is not a dress rehearsal. I refuse to defer living life to its fullest until some future time when I get my money situation straightened out. Without my dreams, my recovery will be bleak at best. I am confident that combining my life's work with my dreams will be a source of genuine happiness and, in turn, will bring success.

New Attitude #8: I will search out true sources of happiness and will practice thankfulness.

I acknowledge that true happiness is found in the infinitely precious things that may not be taken from me. I will look for my joy and contentment in what is permanent, and I will find my anchor in the fact that the God of the universe loves and cares for me, that He sent His only Son to die for me so that I can know I have eternal life. As I see the bigger picture, my day-to-day money issues will diminish and pale in the light of what is truly important.

I know it is impossible to feel self-pity and thankfulness at the same time. The best way I can let go of worry and self-pity is to practice thankfulness. I will create my own personal and specific thankfulness list. I will begin thinking in terms of my blessings that money cannot buy, such as my faith, family, friendships, health, and freedom.

My thankfulness list will become something permanent and precious in my life. During the downtimes (which will inevitably visit me from time to time because I am human), I will reach for my constantly growing thankfulness list instead of the credit cards.

New Attitude #9: I will regularly share my resources with others.

Recognizing that all I have is given to me by God, I commit to give back a portion of my money to His work and share my resources with those who are in need. I will do so joyfully and wisely, knowing that I am entrusted with resources and charged with the responsibility to use them to help others. I will give out of obedience and gratitude, not expecting anything in return.

New Attitude #10: I commit to do whatever it takes and make whatever sacrifices are necessary to achieve and maintain solvency.

I understand that desperate situations often require drastic measures. I am willing to make the adjustments necessary to live within my means. My goal is to achieve personal solvency: That condition where I give generously, save consistently, pay my bills, fulfill my obligations, and still have some left over.

Your past behaviors with money are likely the result of habits. You've repeated the same things over and over and thought the same thoughts about finances so many times that these habits are deep-seated. But it is possible to break bad habits and dump wrong attitudes and replace them with attitudes and behaviors that are in line with God's principles and that bring glory to His name.

Ask God for the wisdom and ability necessary to change your heart and behaviors in the area of your personal finances. As James 1:5 says, "If any of you lacks wisdom, he should ask God, who gives generously to all without finding fault, and it will be given to him." God's promises never fail. As you seek His wisdom and guidance, He will transform your unhealthy attitudes into healthy ones.

The Debt Mess

*How You Got Here and How
to Begin Getting Out*

No one is born in debt . . . yet. I suppose the day may come when each baby who comes into the world will be weighed, measured, fingerprinted, given a Social Security number, and assigned a portion of the national debt. I am thankful that the day has not yet arrived. The bad news is that most of us don't need the government to plunge us into debt—we manage to do that on our own.

If you are an average American, you have four credit cards. These plastic cards have become the standard passport into the vast world of shopping centers, mail-order catalogs, restaurants, transportation, and now even supermarkets and grocery stores.

For some reason, we have come to accept that if the application is approved, the amount of the credit limit becomes cash we're entitled to. If an auto loan is approved, it's as if a mandate has come from on high assuring us that this is certainly an affordable purchase. (It made sense to me. Why would the bank or credit company approve my loan if they didn't know I could repay it? After all, they're the experts.) We are a nation controlled by debt. As of this writing, overall consumer debt in the United States totals more than $1 trillion, a sum that exceeds the annual economic output of many nations. Americans from all economic walks of life are sinking into their own black holes of debt, going into hock for everything from Baccarat crystal to breakfast cereal. The average American household has seven active credit cards with an average outstanding balance of $1,980 per card.[1]

So what exactly is *debt?* Debt is what results when one person owes money to another person, place, or thing. In the strictest sense of the word, owing "a cup of sugar" or "your deepest gratitude" could be construed as a debt; hence the phrase, "I am indebted to your generosity." But for the sake of this book, we'll limit our discussion to *monetary* debt.

There are two kinds of monetary debt—*secured* and *unsecured*. A secured debt involves something tangible to which the lender holds ownership until the debt is completely paid. This tangible property, also called collateral, is typically real estate or automobiles. An unsecured debt is based upon the signature or promise of the borrower. Paying for clothes with a credit card results in an unsecured debt. If you fail to make your credit card payment, the clothes police do not come out and repossess the articles.

For all practical purposes, secured debt is safe debt and not the subject of this chapter. Unsecured debt got me into trouble. This kind of debt is controlling the lives of countless families and individuals in this country.

The difference between secured and unsecured debt has nothing to do with honor, intent, or good faith. There are certain circumstances over which we have no control, such as sudden unemployment, prolonged illness, or the unexpected need of a friend or family member. In the case of a failure to repay a secured loan, or a safe debt, the lender retains ownership of the secured property and the loan is considered repaid. In the case of unsecured debt, the creditor is out of luck. Your promise to pay is worthless, and he is left with no choice but to come after your credit rating.

Excellent financial principles throughout the ages are like the laws of nature—universal and unchanging. To "let no debt remain outstanding" (Romans 13:8) has always been the preferred way to live; that's because the borrower is always the servant to the lender (Proverbs 22:7). Unsecured consumer debt places the debtor in bondage, and as the amount of debt increases, the shackles that bind the enslaved become tighter and heavier. We only deceive ourselves when we acquire goods and services through the use of credit cards and unsecured loans. We pretend that these things liberate us and make our lives fuller. The truth is that we just dig a pit, then jump in and cover ourselves with the weight of the debt. While we would be quick to concur that our heart's desire is to provide an income stream for the future, we are doing just the opposite.

We spend every cent we have, and when there isn't enough (like every month!), the credit cards bridge the gap. For the 72 percent of people who don't pay off the credit card balances every month, the debt begins to build. The next month something unexpected happens, and again the credit cards become lifesavers. Before long, making the minimum payments becomes more and more burdensome, requiring some other creative financing plan such as a debt consolidation loan or another credit card.

Do you see what is happening here? We pledge *future* income—yet unearned—for *current* expenses. Then it becomes next year's salary that will be required to pay this year's expenses. And it is likely that income of the next decade will be required to cover the expenses of the current decade!

Debt doesn't always come in the form of four- and five-figure loans.

I incurred most of our debt a tiny bit at a time. A new outfit here, a nice dinner there, a weekend away because we "deserved" it, cash advances to cover unexpected car repairs . . . and on it went.

In fact, for most people, going into debt starts small and innocently with just a few dollars owed to a friend or family member. Next comes a credit card. Tiny little balances don't seem to be a problem. That $250 stereo is nothing more than $10 a month. Then comes another card and a few minor emergencies. Before long, the debting becomes routine, a pattern that cannot be reversed in a single month.

Common Ways Debt Is Incurred

- Taking a cash advance on a credit card
- Purchasing fuel with a gasoline card
- Requesting an advance on your paycheck, bonus, or commission
- Paying for meals with a credit card
- Putting airline tickets on a credit card
- Buying mail-order items using a credit card
- Failing to pay the rent on time (you owe it, so a debt is created)
- Making arrangements with a hospital, doctor, or dentist to make payments for services rendered

---

Nothing on the above list seems excessive or unusual, does it? Millions of people "debt" in these and similar ways, week in and week out. What's more, we are encouraged to do so. Most of us are pressured on a daily basis to buy on credit and to accept new credit cards and unsecured loans.

Several years ago, when we paid off another (of the many) of our department store credit cards, I got a private moment of glee imagining the horror on the face of the computer operator who entered that last payment. I'm sure panic spread through the department when it finally sank in that for the first time in 22 years the Hunt account showed a zero balance.

My fantasy turned to reality when two weeks later we received two brand-new gold cards from this store with a new-and-improved credit limit of $2,150. The letter from the company's president applauded our most-favored standing! Not only did they send the new cards, but the credit officers offered a 25 percent discount on the first purchase made with the card in addition to "a lovely gift." They're no dummies—they know that if they can get me to use the gold cards once, chances are I'll be hooked again and they can rest easy. I hope they can get over their disappointment.

When our son Jeremy graduated from high school, an exciting piece of mail arrived in our mailbox. Imagine how proud he was to be notified that he had been preapproved for a Visa card. The only thing required was his signature. The bank offering the card painted a solemn picture of the young man away at college with an emergency of dire proportions. The conclusion of the sales pitch was: *Now that you're going to be away from home, you need to be prepared to face life's little emergencies.* The letter went on to point out how expensive books and supplies can be, and how comforting it is to know that you can eliminate worry by simply accepting the credit card. It sounded so wholesome, wise, and mature to plan ahead and be prepared for any predicament that might arise. Yes, it's wise to plan ahead, but plunging oneself into debt is not the way to do it.

Warning Signs of Impending Financial Doom

- Not paying bills on time

- Writing out the checks but waiting to mail them

- Rarely balancing the checking account

- Taking cash advances from credit lines or individuals

- Accepting additional credit cards

- Paying only the minimum on charge accounts

- Bouncing checks

- Borrowing from family and friends

If you are in debt, it probably didn't happen overnight. And getting out won't happen overnight either. I challenge you to resolve right now that you will not debt even one more dollar. Ever. I can't tell you that it will be easy, but I know you can do it. Clearing away the dark clouds of debt will release joy, passion, and excitement in your life.

Peer Pressure

Haven't you always considered peer pressure to be something that plagues only children and adolescents? Harold and I have always tried to teach our boys that peer pressure, if not recognized, could persuade them to participate in unwise or destructive behaviors only because "everyone else is doing it." We want our children to demonstrate control over the pressure of their peers and feel they should be able to weigh, measure, and make the right choices based upon their own value system. We tell them to stand up for what they know is right; just because everyone else is doing it doesn't mean they have to.

Such training is probably not effective if kids see their parents living to "one-up" and "keep up with" their friends and peers. Have you ever considered that you might be accepting behaviors from yourself that you'd never tolerate in your kids? Many adults succumb to peer pressure, only in ways different from the ways young people do. Just think of all the ways our lives are shaped and defined by peer pressure: how and where our kids are educated; the size and location of our homes; the model and year of our automobiles; the labels on our clothing; the magnitude and originality of birthday parties; the lavishness and immensity of Christmas; and on and on. . . .

Depending on your motivation, there may be nothing wrong with these things in and of themselves; the problem occurs when debting becomes the only way to acquire and peer pressure justifies the act.

Perma-Debt

Issuers of credit cards have only one agenda: to keep us permanently in debt. Their mission is to put out the bait (the preapproved card), jerk the hook (offering an attractive interest rate, rebate, or gift on the first use), and reel us in. The rest is easy. They know that if the average person can be enticed to accept a credit card and use it just once, he or she will remain hooked for 15 years or more.

Consumer credit interest rates are sky-high, anywhere from, say, 16 percent to 22 percent. But taking into account an annual fee, an over-credit-line fee, a cash-advance fee, and many other fees, some cards are effectively charging more like 30 percent interest. When you think in these terms, it's pretty hard to understand why anyone thinks that being a card-holder is a privilege.

Consumer credit is a big-time industry. The credit card companies and banks have much at stake. Your perma-debt situation is their lifeblood, and you can be sure they are quite interested in maintaining that condition.

Should You Cut Up All Your Credit Cards?

It would be wonderful not to carry any credit cards—then the means through which most debt is accumulated would be eliminated. But in these high-tech, electronic times, every family needs one all-purpose credit card (only one!). It will come in handy if you need to rent a car, secure a hotel room, or book airline tickets over the phone. However—and listen carefully—the balance *must* be paid off during the grace period or the activity turns into debting, and you know how dangerous that is.

If you don't trust yourself to carry a credit card, try this: Fill an empty coffee can half-full with water, and freeze it. Then place your credit card on top of the ice and fill to the top with water, and return the can to your freezer. The card will be available if you *absolutely* need it, but the time required to thaw your ice cube card will make it difficult to use and at least will give you time to reconsider any purchase you want to make with it.

Bouncing Checks

A checking account can be a clever way to acquire things when you're broke. I used to do it, so I know the difference between an honest mistake and a planned, contrived manipulation. There is a law against passing bad checks. Criminal prosecution is generally reserved for habitual offenders or people with criminal intent. If these criteria don't apply to you, chances are you don't need to worry about being jailed for it. Instead, you get to pay huge punitive damages. As of this writing, $30 a pop per bounced check is not unusual in many areas.

The way I see it, overdraft penalties are unconscionably large interest rates on money borrowed for a short period of time. Another problem arises, however, for the perpetual check bouncer: Creditors and merchants don't trust people who bounce checks.

If you have never had a problem with bouncing checks, you're to be admired. If, on the other hand, you have experienced this problem first-hand, you've probably felt the shame that goes along with it. The whole concept of the checking account was developed to fulfill a need for convenience and safety—not to be used as a loan vehicle. If you know the embarrassment of having an account closed involuntarily due to excessive overdraft activity, you would do well to heed my advice and do whatever it takes to change your ways. Here are some tips:

- *Record every transaction.* I can almost hear some of you checkbook-perfectionist types laughing, but many of us have difficulty doing this. You see, once the expenditure is written down, it becomes real. Until such time, a state of denial can be quite comfortable. As long as the current balance remains a "guesstimate," you feel as if you can continue spending with reckless abandon. It's amazing how that guesstimate balance is rarely close to the real amount. Make yourself write down every check, every deposit, and the current balance —every transaction at the moment it occurs. And don't forget transactions at the automatic teller machines (ATMs). Write them in your checking account register at the time you make the withdrawal.

- *As much as possible, live with cash.* There are times when you will need to write checks, as when you send funds through the mail. But in your day-to-day living, dealing with cash will revolutionize your financial life. When you leave the house in the morning and take only the amount of cash you'll need for the day, you won't be tempted to write checks for things you don't need or can't afford.

• *Stay away from slippery places.* Don't hang around the mall or pore over mail-order catalogs. Don't set yourself up for a fall if you are easily influenced to believe you need everything you see.

How to Begin Climbing Out of the Hole

This entire book is about getting out of debt, learning to manage money responsibly, and gaining financial freedom. So you will find lots of ideas and strategies in the following chapters. For now, however, let's look at a few first steps that you can begin to take to climb out of the debt hole.

Commit to Honesty

When your financial life is all messed up, every area of life is affected. Even your basic value system is vulnerable and open to attack. There are few areas that challenge your integrity as much as financial pressure. That's why such phrases as these have come into being: "The check's in the mail"; "I mailed it, so if it doesn't show up, I'll stop payment and send another"; and (to a department store clerk) "There must be some mistake; I paid my account in full just last week!" Or maybe you've heard yourself or someone else say, "My check bounced? Oh, the bank screwed up my account. Just redeposit it." Need I go on?

As I mentioned in the last chapter, you must develop an attitude of honesty and integrity if you're going to get out of your mess and into the black. Make a pact between God and yourself that you are going to approach your finances with complete and brutal honesty. Let creditors with whom you've been less than honest in the past know that you are embarking on a financial recovery plan.

Stop Debting

I understand that using the word *debt* (noun) as a verb (to debt) is rather unscholarly and grammatically incorrect. You won't find *debting* in the dictionary. But I like to use it because *debting* sounds wrong and it *is* wrong. *Debting* has come to mean the act of owing money to another. To debt is the action of incurring a debt, as in *I debt, you debt, we debt* . . . you get the picture.

Debting can involve a personal loan from a parent or child; it can be unpaid rent or an installment purchase that does not involve collateral or one of who-knows-how-many other ways of getting something without paying for it now. These days, debting most commonly happens with a credit card. Consumer credit is rather plentiful, available in just about every retail store in the country. And the availability of that credit has plunged the vast majority of adult Americans into terrible debt. It has become the norm to spend what we do not have, and we are not the only ones to do it—look at our national debt. (I wouldn't dare quote a figure, for indeed it would be incorrect by the time this sentence is finished!)

Everywhere we turn, we're encouraged to buy what we want now, regardless of whether or not we have enough in cash or savings to pay for it, let alone need it. We are encouraged to do it on credit—to buy now and pay (a lot more) later, including outrageous interest rates. Creditors often want to lull debtors into a false sense of security, the said state of mind being conducive to buying things debtors would, on cooler reflection, see they couldn't afford.

Compulsive debting is more than just an occasional meal charged on a bank card. It is the repeated use of credit, first by choice and later by necessity. In time, a big chunk of discretionary income is required to pay the minimum payments on the charge cards, and so when an unexpected expense rears its ugly head, the debtor feels there is no choice but to incur yet another debt. And then the monthly payments are that much greater, causing that much more pressure. And so it goes. Eventually, the credit sources will become "maxed out," but rarely in the case of a compulsive debtor will that stop the activity. A new way to debt will be found, and the problem just grows and grows.

There's only one way to reverse this process: Stop. The best way to make sure you stop is to cut up the cards, cancel the accounts, and commit to the fastest payoff schedule possible. This is serious business, and stopping may very well be one of the hardest things you will ever do.

I'll not soon forget the day I was able to part with my cards. I felt stripped, naked, and violated. But one hour at a time I was able to get hold of myself, and within a relatively short period of time that empty, worthless feeling was replaced with one of freedom and relief. Isn't it wonderful how God has a way of filling our inadequacies with His power and strength?

Keep a Spending Record

We teach our children from a young age how to respect our privacy, and as they mature, their own rights to privacy are bestowed upon them. Little by little they become more self-governing and less accountable to outsiders until one day the fully matured, independent little birds are ready to leave the nest to make it on their own. Somewhere in that journey from the nest to the new nesting grounds, the transfer of accountability from parent to self should take place.

But in the area of finances, the process must have a high rate of breakdown because too many of us end up accountable to no one for our personal finances. And that aversion to accountability is our worst enemy. Example: Have you any idea of your average cost for food per month during the last year? How much you spend on utilities in the average month? Auto repairs? Cab fare? What is the total amount of money you spent last month to service your debts? What percentage of that went toward debt reduction? What did you spend in coffee shops and on fast food . . . yesterday? Don't feel too bad—the typical person has a difficult time coming up with anything close to exact figures for such routine expenses.

I suppose denial has something to do with it. If you have no idea what your bank balance is, it is easy to play games and fool yourself by adding a digit or two instead of facing the possible reality that you don't have enough in there to buy a newspaper, let alone cover the cash advance you managed to pull out of the automatic teller machine last night.

Assuming you are sick and tired of living in a financial fog, not knowing where all the money goes, then you desperately need the brilliant light that only a precise spending record will turn on in your life. You may be hesitant to bring into sharp focus the exact nature of your finances. And just like a strong new pair of eyeglasses that correct fuzzy vision, there will be a period of adjustment. You may even develop a headache. But you cannot overestimate the value and importance of recording your spending. Knowing the truth will set you free.

Here's how to get started: For the next 30 days, keep a Daily Spending Record. A spending record is simply a written accounting for money spent, including funds withdrawn from the automatic teller machine. And for now, keeping this record should not necessarily entail any changes in spending activity. You need to know how you spend your money, and this is the only way to find out. If you are part of a couple in which one person handles the bulk of the money, this is going to require a little teamwork. If you have an uncooperative partner, start by becoming accountable to yourself for whatever amount of money you control.

Get yourself a notebook or pad of paper, something small and practical. Each day, start with a fresh page and put the current date at the top. Each time you spend cash or write a check, jot down two entries: what for and how much. That's it. One page per day, every day. No time off. No endless details and no totals (for now).

Typical Daily Spending Record

Date:

Tommy's lunch	$ 1.35
Coffee (2)	$ .50
Lunch	$ 3.78
Grocery store	$ 28.73
Rent	$ 550.00
Gasoline	$ 10.00
Jenny's school supplies	$ 2.34

At the end of the first week, gather up your seven individual records and merge them into one record, a Weekly Spending Record. I'm certain you'll be able to come up with a format that works perfectly for you, and it may not be exactly like mine. No matter how it looks, make sure that your record includes everything you've spent in the week, including checks you've written. Please don't make this more difficult than it is.

Typical Weekly Spending Record

Week #1

Savings	$100.00
Groceries	$83.46
Food (away from home)	$52.73
Rent	$550.00
Telephone	$68.74
Gasoline	$20.00
Oil change/lube	$14.95
Clothing	$53.87
Kids' miscellaneous	$5.86
Gifts (Grandma's birthday)	$9.58
Household maint. (Home Depot)	$38.68
Magazines/subscriptions	$12.95
Newspapers	$1.75
Total Week #1	$1012.57

The next step is to develop four Weekly Spending Records into a Monthly Spending Record. The final step will be to develop your customized Monthly Spending Plan. But in order to do that, you will need the information coming up in chapters 7, 8, and 9.

Your assignment until we pick up this subject again in chapter 9 is to get comfortable with keeping Daily Spending Records and turning them into Weekly Spending Records every seven days.

Start Saving

Experts tell us that everyone should have cash put away to cover at least six months of expenses. When you are on the edge, that thought usually brings a sarcastic retort: "Yeah, right!" The goal line can seem a million miles away to someone starting on his own one-yard line. So start by having enough to cover one week, then move to a pay period and then one month. At that point at least you will have enough to live on until your unemployment checks kick in. Each time you make a savings deposit, you will be backing away from the edge, and that feels so good. (Chapter 6 will go into more detail on the best ways to start saving.)

Debt Keeps Us Living on the Edge

Whenever I think of the phrase "life on the edge," I am propelled into childhood memories involving family automobile trips, great heights, and narrow roads. Without fail, I was always on the side of the car closest to the edge. And my front-row seat gave me a spectacular view of the bottomless canyon below with its giant mouth open, ready to swallow me up in the event I dared to come one inch closer. Add to that the perilous thought that I had absolutely no control over the situation, partly because I was a child but mostly because I couldn't reach the steering wheel or brake. One swerve, one jerk of the steering wheel and our car would have plummeted to disaster. I often thought how much more comfortable I could be if I were on the safe side of the car and my brother next to the edge—that way he would go first and break my fall.

Not until we were safe at last on the straight, flat, boring highway could I relax and enjoy the trip. How sad that I missed so much of the beauty because all I could think about was falling off the edge.

Like those fearful car trips riding on the brink of disaster, living on the edge of financial ruin is precarious and anxiety-producing. Never having enough money to pay all of the bills, postdating a check or two, writing checks in hopes they won't clear until your next paycheck is deposited, committing next week's paycheck for this week's expenses, wondering how you would pay your bills if you lost your job tomorrow—all of these things keep you living on the edge.

Living under this kind of gloominess can be depressing to say the least. The worst part is that so much energy is expended worrying and fretting that the beauty and joy of the moment are lost in the glare of stress and strain. But you don't have to live month after month feeling that if you come one inch closer, you will fall and be swallowed up by the jaws of financial ruin. Beginning with the simple steps we've discussed in this chapter and following the strategies outlined in the rest of this book will help you gain the peace of mind to enjoy the journey through life.

1. Figures taken from RAM Research Group, Frederick, Md., and *USA Today*, May 28, 1996.

Chapter 5

The Principle of Giving

Expose Yourself to
Supernatural Intervention

I hope you're not about to do what I fear you might—skip this chapter. I say that only because I know myself and I'm quite sure that's exactly what I might have done when my financial life was all messed up. Why should I waste my time reading what I already know I should do—and have such a hard time doing?

I grew up in church. I'm not exaggerating. As the daughter of a pastor in a medium-sized community, I spent many, many hours each week in some kind of church setting, starting nine months before my birth and lasting until I left home.

Believe me when I say I've heard a lot of sermons, many of which were on the subject of tithing and stewardship. As a kid, I knew this tithing stuff so well I could have preached a compelling message on the subject, including flawless recitations of appropriate Scriptures. The problem is, the truth of that knowledge got stuck in my head. It didn't find its way into my heart until many years later.

I say all this to assure you that what follows isn't from my head—it's from my heart.

I get the same question over and over when people learn that I managed to run up an incredible six-figure amount of unsecured debt: "How did you ever pay it all back?!" My answer always startles the questioners, because given the world's standards, it is about the dumbest tactic one could think of. I reply, "We started giving away some of our money." Another way to put it is, we started obeying God's laws and following the guidelines set forth in Scripture. I don't know that I've ever felt such gratitude as I did in those early years of our financial recovery. I was so thankful to have money coming in at all that giving part of it to God was a pleasure.

A funny thing began to happen. More money came in. Greater opportunities presented themselves for me to earn even more, which allowed us to start paying back the debts rapidly. As I look back, I am astounded by the ways God put the pieces of our financial puzzle back together. I couldn't really see it at the time, so it was pure trust that drove me to give.

God gave me an opportunity to enter the field of real estate at a time when it was a hot industry in Southern California. I had no special education or experience to open those doors. I wasn't a member of a prestigious family with great wealth and standing in the community. And the oddest thing of all, I am, obviously, a woman and the industrial/commercial real estate industry was—and continues to be—a male-dominated field. There was no reason, humanly speaking, that I should have ever been accepted, let alone found success, in that industry. I have no doubt that God blessed my heart's desire to change, pay back the debt, and obey Him in this area of giving.

You've probably heard it a thousand times, but I'll make it a thousand and one: It's impossible to out-give God. I believe that with all my heart, because I have proven it over and over again.

Let's be careful here: I am not saying we should give to get. There are some misguided teachers who say that if we will just give enough, we will absolutely, guaranteed get tenfold in return from God. But that's nothing more than an attempt to manipulate God. Instead, we give to God first and foremost because that is what He's asked us to do. We give out of obedience to Him. Having said that, I think everyone who makes a habit of giving would agree that blessings follow when we generously share our resources with others. The blessings might come in the form of joy and satisfaction, new opportunities or whatever.

The act of giving itself is fabulous, but it has many side benefits as well:

- Giving to God is an act of worship. By offering to God the best of what we have with hearts full of love and gratitude, we are worshiping the One who provides for all our needs. We acknowledge that God is the creator of all and that our very existence depends on Him.

- Giving to God is to trust. I can't say I actually understand how this works—how it is that in giving we receive—but I have seen it in operation time after time. Giving out of your abundance is an act of thanksgiving, but giving out of your need is an act of faith. "He who gives to the poor will lack nothing, but he who closes his eyes to them receives many curses" (Proverbs 28:27).

- Giving to God promotes humility. By sharing our money with others—rather than hoarding it and holding it with clenched fists—we acknowledge that what we have really belongs to God, not us. We are entrusted with resources and charged with the responsibility to use them to help others. Nothing will quiet our greed and cure a case of the "I-wants" like giving away part of our income.

- Giving to God helps us find balance. The perfect formula for creating balance in your finances is to give away 10 percent, save 10 percent, and then learn to live within the 80 percent that's left. I love the way those figures fit together—it's all so tidy and orderly. While this is a wonderful formula, let me say that there's nothing magical about giving 10 percent. That is, I believe we should give as we've been given. So as you attain greater and greater financial freedom, you may choose to pass along more and more of your money to those in need.

- Giving to God is a demonstration of gratitude. We give to God because we love Him and we're grateful beyond belief for all that He has done for us. Giving from a thankful heart and expecting nothing in return is a sweet offering to the One who owns everything anyway. It's the least we can do.

How much of our income to give away and to whom are personal decisions that each of us must make according to God's leading. Nevertheless, let me suggest some guidelines to help you through the decision-making process:

1. *Give first.* If you deposit your income into the bank, go about your weekly activities, and intend to take care of giving later, you probably won't. I suggest that you make up some payment coupons similar to those you have for your mortgage payment. Put them at the front of your bills-to-be-paid folder to ensure that making that payment is the first thing you do. As Proverbs 3:9-10 says, "Honor the Lord with your wealth, with the *firstfruits* of all your crops [or paycheck]; then your barns will be filled to overflowing, and your vats will brim over with new wine" (emphasis added). Giving will become a habit provided you repeat the act over and over.

2. *Give wisely.* I suggest that if you are part of a church you should support that ministry financially because that is where you are being fed spiritually. When considering other charitable organizations or ministries, first request a current financial report. Learn what they are doing, how they do it, and who is in charge. I am suspicious of any organization that is not open with its financial affairs and any whose overheard and administrative costs

exceed 25 percent. In other words, at least 75 cents of every dollar I give should make it to the actual work I wish to support.

3. *Give quietly.* Don't trumpet the fact that you give money away. Give because it is the right thing to do and because you are grateful for all that's been given to you—not because you want other people to admire your generosity and benevolence. Keep in mind Jesus' words: "When you give to the needy, do not announce it with trumpets, as the hypocrites do in the synagogues and on the streets, to be honored by men. I tell you the truth, they have received their reward in full. But when you give to the needy, do not let your left hand know what your right hand is doing, so that your giving may be in secret. Then your Father, who sees what is done in secret, will reward you" (Matthew 6:2-4).

4. *Give joyfully.* You may not feel all that obedient or grateful when you begin to follow this principle of giving. That's okay. Ask God to make your heart joyful and just keep giving. The feelings of joy will come. It's much easier to act your way into a feeling than to feel your way into action. "Each man should give what he has decided in his heart to give, not reluctantly or under compulsion, for God loves a cheerful giver" (2 Corinthians 9:7).

When you are worried, filled with anxiety, or just feeling greedy, give! It is the best all-purpose remedy I know for money troubles. The following account by Dr. Norman Vincent Peale is a wonderful illustration of the blessings that come from giving.

Back in 1930, I was a young married minister in Syracuse, New York. My salary, which had been a handsome (in those days) $6,000 a year, was cut twice—first to $5,000, then to $4,000. We had no manse or home supplied by the church. Everyone was frightened and depressed. Businesses were failing. Nobody could borrow money; there was no money to be had. Men used to greet one another grimly by saying, "Have you had your pay cut yet?" Everyone had to take several cuts before that depression ended, and many people lost their jobs altogether.

With a salary of $4,000 a year, I just didn't see how we could get by. My salary was the only income we had. I was helping my younger brother with college expenses, and I knew he had to count on that. The pressure got worse and worse. I hated to burden Ruth [my wife] with my fears. One night I went out alone and walked through Walnut Park near our little apartment, and for the first time in my life I felt icy terror clutching at my mind and heart. I was terrified. When I finally went home, I said to Ruth, "We're in a desperate situation. We can't pay the bills. What are we going to do?"

And her answer really startled me. She said, "We're going to start tithing."

"Tithing?" I echoed. "We can't! It's impossible!"

"Not impossible," Ruth said. "Essential. You know what the Old Testament promises to those who give 10 percent of everything to the Lord." I can see her yet, standing in the kitchen and quoting, "Bring ye all the tithes into the storehouse . . . and prove Me now herewith said the Lord of hosts, if I will not open you the windows of heaven and pour you out a blessing that there shall not be room enough to receive it" (Malachai 3:10).

"We're going to do that," she said stoutly, "because tithing is an act of faith and the Bible says that if we have faith even as small as a grain of mustard seed, nothing will be impossible for us. We have to start imagining God's prosperity."

So we did it. And Ruth was right. Money didn't pour in, but there always was enough. Furthermore, the act of tithing calmed my fears and stimulated my mind so that I began thinking. I started imagining. I knew I had one small talent: public speaking. And so I offered myself as a public speaker wherever one was needed. I spoke at civic clubs and garden clubs and graduations and community gatherings. Sometimes I was paid five or 10 dollars, sometimes nothing at all. But it helped. What a thrill I felt when I received the first $25 fee. Then someone who heard me speak offered me a chance to go on radio. Again, I received no money for this, but the number of speaking invitations increased. So one thing led to another and gradually we began to get our heads above water.

I am convinced that tithing did it. Ruth and I have been tithers ever since. Through the years in sermons and talks I have recommended tithing to thousands of people and hundreds have been persuaded to try it. Of those hundreds, not one has ever told me that the experiment failed, that he regretted it, or that it was a mistake. Not a single person.

It's almost as if there is an invisible reservoir of abundance in the universe that can be tapped if you will just obey certain spiritual laws. The word abundance, I'm told, comes from a Latin phrase meaning to "rise up in waves." When you tithe, it does seem as if little waves of abundance start rising up all around you.

So if you have financial difficulties, face up to them not just with courage and intelligence, but also with warmhearted generosity and concern for others.[1]

1. Quoted by permission of *Plus* magazine, vol. 40, no. 4 (Part III), May 1989. Copyright © 1989 by the Foundation for Christian Living, P.O. Box FCL, Pawling, NY 12564; (914) 855-5000.

Chapter 6

The Principle of Saving

Part of Everything You Earn Is Yours to Keep

You must save for the future. Part of everything you earn is yours to keep—not to sock away so you can buy a new sofa or remodel the kitchen, but yours to *keep* so it will grow and multiply and be available to you in the future. Properly managed, money you save will start working for you, slowly at first, but eventually as hard as you would ever expect an employee to work. And then it will reproduce itself to do the work of two employees and then three, four, and even more.

Right now you may be throwing up your hands and writing me off as a total idiot who thinks you can somehow save money you don't even have. But hold on. I do understand. People in financial difficulty don't save money. That's because we save whatever is *left over* after our month's expenses are met, and those of us in financial trouble never have anything left over! Not so hard to figure. After all, we are so busy spending next month's income that the thought of saving anything hardly crosses our minds.

Saving is something we'll do someday when we win the lottery. It's something we'll do someday when we get a big inheritance. It's something we'll do someday when we have an extra $2,000 to get started. Someday, someday, someday. The truth is that a part of everything you earn is yours to keep *right now*.

When you look at your paycheck, do you get a sick feeling in the pit of your stomach because it is so small and every stinkin' cent is spoken for? Well, my friend, that's going to change. It has to! Your goal is to eventually save 10 percent of everything you earn. Can you really do it? Of course you can!

Don't Leave It to Chance

Your savings plan needs to be formal and consistent. "Formal" means a predetermined, fixed amount. It doesn't matter what amount you start with—it can be $.50 or $50—but it should be at least the same amount every time. "Consistent" means the same time every week, every two weeks, every month, or whatever. If you save a set amount at a set time, then you have a formal and consistent savings program.

Studies show that anyone with an annual income of $10,000 or more has *some* discretionary money. That's it. You have no more excuses. For you, saving money is indeed a choice. You can choose to or choose not to. But you can no longer say you can't.

The best way to save is to have money automatically moved into your savings account. Hard as it is to believe, what you don't see you don't miss. So having your savings deducted before you ever see your check is the way to go. This can be done through regular payroll deductions or through your bank, which will transfer money from your checking account into your savings. And you can instruct your bank to make automatic deposits into an investment account, such as a certificate of deposit (CD).

A part of everything you earn is yours to keep. That just has to be one of the sweetest sentences in the English language. I need to keep repeating it because you need to keep hearing it. Notice: I said "yours to keep."

Watch It Grow

Eventually, this savings program is going to start growing for you, just like a tiny seed that is planted, watered, and tended and then becomes strong, secure, and solid. The roots of your "savings tree" will be deep, and you will feel protected.

If you dare, think about all the interest you've paid on your debts and how much more you're going to have to pay before you become debt-free. Kinda makes you sick, doesn't it? Saving money takes that same principle and makes it work to your advantage. Instead of taking money from you for debt interest, a savings account pays you money.

Example: Jerry begins a formal and consistent savings program on his twenty-first birthday. He saves $50 each month like clockwork. If he earns just 6 percent interest during his working years, his $26,400 total investment will grow to $129,859 by the time he retires at age 65. If the same amount earns an average of 12 percent interest (certainly not unthinkable), Jerry will have $960,949. Of course, he will owe tax on the interest somewhere along the line, but that's still almost $1 million, thanks to the miracle of compounding interest.

Interest rates rise and fall just like mountain highways. If you get discouraged when rates drop into the valley and decide 2 or 3 percent interest is just not worth the trip, you may never experience the breathtaking mountaintop experiences. You must be committed to a savings plan for the long haul. Don't worry about the interest rate today; your concern should be the average rate of interest compounded over a long period of time.

If you are a math whiz or if you have a calculator handy, figure what the compounded interest will do if you save 10 percent of your annual income starting now until you retire. Here's an example: Your average annual income is $50,000, and you save 10 percent ($5,000) each year in an investment that earns 10 percent interest compounded for 35 years. Your nest egg will become $1,595,115 before taxes, even though you will contribute only $175,000. And that does not take into consideration any raises you will get over 35 years. It's a miracle, folks.

You've experienced the devastating growth rate of debts. You know how interest has compounded against you and loaded you down with a burden of anxiety. Well, it's time you see the miracle of compounded interest when it is growing in your favor. The secret to the miracle of compounded interest is in saving consistently, every week, every month. Slow growth is the key. This miracle is available to anyone. And if you can't start with 10 percent, start with $10, or $.10. Just start. When you are putting something away for yourself, choosing to deny yourself in another area won't seem so unreasonable.

While the sugar bowl or cookie jar in the kitchen cupboard might be a good place to stash the cash in the beginning, I don't recommend that approach for very long. That cash is simply too easy to dip into, and you won't earn interest on it. But do your homework before you open a bank account. Many banks have ridiculous fees and minimum balances on regular savings accounts, so check around for the best banking arrangement. Many credit unions have no-fee savings accounts.

Get into the habit of feeding the account regularly, but don't get into the habit of checking on it every week. It's like the watched pot that never boils. The benefit to you right now is not in the balance in your bank book but in the new attitude you've developed. You've made a 180-degree change in the direction you were heading!

Reap the Rewards

Saving money brings many benefits. Whereas previously you felt naked, scared, and vulnerable to life's curveballs, you will soon begin to feel more secure and protected. Putting money away in a bank or investment account may be the most addictive thing you've ever done (a good kind of addiction!). You see your savings account growing, and you can't wait to see it grow even more.

Saving makes you feel that you're getting a handle on life. You begin to feel responsible and able to cope because you have a better "vision." You are not stuck in the moment but are able to see the big picture and how your savings will give you security in the future. Saving money promotes maturity and self-discipline. It really does have a snowball effect. Saving on a consistent basis is probably the best antidote to out-of-control spending and one of the best gifts you could give yourself. Listen to two readers who put this principle into practice:

> You said to save at least 10 percent of our income for the future. My husband and I just started last June, and now we have over $3,000 socked away. I put the money in a savings account that's off-limits. We never touch it. I want to thank you because while I've always been a good saver, we've always spent with the best of them, too, and this 10 percent off the top prevents us from frittering away all our extra money.
>
> —Sue

> For years I limped by from paycheck to paycheck, never having any cushion. But I listened to your advice and asked my bank to take 10 percent of my monthly deposits out of my checking account and into my savings. Your methods of debt reduction and putting something away for savings no matter what have led me to open a mutual fund while continuing to build my regular savings. What a stress-reliever to have some money tucked away for the future!
>
> —James

Chapter 7

The Principle of Living Debt-Free

*How to Develop Your Rapid
Debt-Repayment Plan*

I t's been several years now since I received the following letter, but it is
still one of the most memorable.

Like a lot of people, I got my first credit card with a feeling of
"having arrived" and declared it "only for emergencies." I still
remember a coworker's laugh when I said that. Five years later, I
had six cards, all maxed out due to "emergencies" and then I
understood what prompted her chuckle. I owe for car repairs on

a car I no longer own; furniture that I sold in a garage sale; braces that came off my son's teeth a year ago; but worst of all, my balances include several thousand dollars' worth of expenses I don't even remember.

Everyone who goes into debt and successfully digs out has a turning point. Mine came when Christmas arrived and I found myself buried in bills with no more room to charge on any cards. I took a job working for minimum wage at a department store for the holidays. My entire Christmas season was miserable because I was exhausted and had no time to enjoy festivities with my family. But it was such a valuable experience that I recommend this to anyone sinking into Credit Card Hell.

Working in that store, I saw credit from a whole different perspective. Customers would make a small payment on a huge balance, charge twice that while they were in the store and pay several times as much in the end on already overpriced merchandise because they had their credit line and no cash reserves. They bought top-of-the-line clothing and housewares to give as gifts in order to keep up appearances but confessed they would never be able to afford these things for themselves. As a cashier, I knew before they got to the register which customers would charge their purchases; they were the ones with the tired, sad expressions, the ones who were obviously not enjoying the holiday season or anything else. I felt guilty suggesting purchases (the training staff at this store instructed us to suggest the highest priced options and sell by pushing low payments while never divulging the number of payments) and putting their selections on account, because I was helping make their lives worse. I even felt bad giving discounts to entice first-time credit card buyers because I knew the merchandise they were buying would not last as long as the payments. The giddy look on newlyweds' faces when they first discovered they had more buying power than cash looked sickeningly familiar. That's the bad news.

The good news is, for the first time in years I made up my

mind to get off that merry-go-round forever. I am now going in the opposite direction—out of the hole instead of deeper in. Since the beginning of the year, I have devised and stuck with a two-year financial recovery plan, and I'm beginning to see real results.

Ironically, I am beginning to feel the same things I felt years ago when I got my first credit card: powerful, in charge, secure, and prepared for emergencies. Only this time, the emotions are based in reality. Thank you again for your wonderful publications.

—McKenzey

If you want to sabotage your Money Makeover, keep on incurring new debts. That's right. Just keep those credit cards charged right up to the max, and as your income increases over the years, make sure you get into as much debt as possible. That way, no matter how much you work at reducing your expenses and saving for the future, your debts will stick with you right to the grave, weighing you down and robbing you of happiness. You can make sure you are just one more person who only dreamed of enjoying wonderful things and seeing beautiful places because you never quite got your money straightened out.

On the other hand, if you are excited about the possibility of changing the way you deal with money, developing new money attitudes, experiencing happiness and satisfaction from knowing how to handle your resources in an intelligent and reasoned way, then it is mandatory you stop incurring debt and reverse that destructive behavior. Designing your own Rapid Debt-Repayment Plan is an important part of your Money Makeover.

Reality Check

Allow me to introduce you to a rarely thought of and even less enjoyable activity called *debt repayment*. This may come as a shock, but your debts have to be repaid somehow, somewhere, sometime. The credit card companies are not in business to supply you with free clothes and fancy meals. That was a big shock to me, too—a terrible reality I had to face. If you are relying on the minimum monthly payments to pay off your debt anytime soon, think again.

Let's say you owe $2,000 on your credit card, which charges 19.8 percent interest for the privilege. Your minimum monthly payment is 3 percent of the outstanding balance, which is presently $60 and fluctuates each month depending on the principal. All that's required is $60, so that's all you pay, right? If you were to make only the minimum payment each month, how long do you think it will take you to pay off that $2,000 if you never make another purchase? I'll tell you: 19 years and four months, assuming your payments are never late and you do not add any new purchases. By the time you finish, you will have paid interest in the amount of $4,318.12. That's $2,000 — plus $4,318.12!

If you are a typical consumer—i.e., a preferred and valued customer, meaning you keep your credit cards "maxed out" or at least make sure there's a good, healthy balance rolling over from month to month—it is highly unlikely your consumer debt will ever be paid off. You will continue to pay this month for food you consumed years ago, clothes you've long since given away, and other stuff you've undoubtedly forgotten about completely. That, my friends, is perma-debt, and the credit card companies love it.

Let's go back to the example of the $2,000 debt, which requires a monthly minimum payment of $60. What if through some stroke of unexplained sense you made a solemn and personal pledge to pay $60 every month until the darned thing was paid in full, choosing to ignore that the actual monthly minimum payment requirement was going down every month? You would reach a zero balance in just 49 months, instead of 232 months (19 years, four months). And if you got really sane and committed to pay $90 a month? The debt would be history in just 28 months. Brace yourself here. Let's assume you *really* lost your mind and made a personal pledge to pay $100 a month against the $2,000 debt. You would pay it off in just 24 months, more than 17 years sooner than if you believed the credit card company when it said all you have to pay is the minimum monthly balance. I never cease to be amazed at the power of compounded interest and what it can do to one's financial picture.

Plan Your Work and Work Your Plan

All of us who are intimately familiar with overspending know that it is very easy to five-and-ten dollar ourselves into oblivion. The good news is that you can five-and-ten dollar yourself right back to financial health, too. The key to rapid debt repayment is to make a plan and stick to it as if your life depended on it. It may. The details of the plan you devise for your own debt reduction are not nearly as important as your determination to carry it out.

There are several methods of rapid debt reduction that work equally well. One method involves a plan whereby each of your debts is paid off proportionately so that they all reach zero balance at the same time.

However, the method I will teach you (and which is, coincidentally, my personal favorite) is based on the principle that it feels good to work extra hard on one bill at a time in order to experience the exhilaration of a zero balance as quickly as possible. Paying off one debt completely gives a great boost to your determination to pay off the next and the next and the next.

While not instant gratification, this method certainly offers short-term achievable goals. Small doses of gratification along the way keep one motivated. Here's how it works:

The first thing you must do is determine exactly how much you owe and the exact nature of your debts. We are talking about unsecured debt— anything that you owe but that would not be subject to repossession if you stopped paying—such as credit card balances, personal loans, payments you are making to the dentist or doctor. Make a list of all of the unsecured debts, outlining the current balance, minimum payment, interest rate, and number of payments required to pay the amount in full. If you do not possess the math skills required to figure how many payments will be required to pay off the debt, use a financial calculator, or call each creditor and ask. With their super computer programs, they should be able to tell you. (However, they may be reluctant to.)

Next, arrange these debts in order of the number of months required to pay in full, with the shortest payoff first on the list. See the "Sam and Samantha Example" chart that follows. The debt they placed first on the list has a balance of $80. With a minimum payment of $35, it will take just a

Sam and Samantha Example's Rapid Debt-Repayment Plan

Debt Free in just 24 months ✳

Creditor	$ Bal	%	1	2	3	4	5	6	7	8	9	10	11	12	13	14	15	16	17	18	19	20	21	22	23	24	25	26	27
Dept. Store #1	80	16.9	35	35	12	0																							
Personal Loan	700	10	108	108	131	143	143	89	0																				
Student Loan	200	6	26	26	26	26	26	74	0																				
Visa #1	1,500	18	108	108	108	108	108	114	277	277	277	277	209	0															
Orthodontist	1,000	18	40	40	40	40	40	40	40	40	40	40	108	385	369	0													
Credit Union	3,000	12	120	120	120	120	120	120	120	120	120	120	120	120	136	437	437	437	437	437	145	0							
Finance Co.	1,200	14	45	45	45	45	45	45	45	45	45	45	45	45	45	45	45	45	45	45	337	278	0						
Mastercard	1,000	19.6	40	40	40	40	40	40	40	40	40	40	40	40	40	40	40	40	40	40	40	244	264	0					
Visa #2	650	18	32	32	32	32	32	32	32	32	32	32	32	32	32	32	32	32	32	32	32	32	128	0					
Dept. Store #2	2,000	18.5	65	65	65	65	65	65	65	65	65	65	65	65	65	65	65	65	65	65	65	65	227	519	0				
Totals	11,330		619	619	619	619	619	619	619	619	619	619	619	619	619	619	619	619	619	619	619	619	619	519	DEBT FREE!				

bit longer than two months to pay it off, which is less than any of their other debts.

Next, add up the total of the current minimum monthly payments. This is an important number, so write it down, embed it in your brain, tattoo it on your forehead, paint it on your walls, teach it to your children. This number for the Examples is $619 each month.

And now . . . it's commitment time. Look again at the total of your minimum monthly payments—the number you've just embedded in your brain. This is the amount of money you must commit to pay toward your Rapid Debt-Repayment Plan until all of your debts are paid. I don't think you should find this at all out of line, because this is the amount you have to pay every month anyway (assuming you don't skip payments). At this time I am not asking you to pay any more than you are required to pay. (It wouldn't be such a bad idea, but it's not required.) This is the minimum amount you must devote to your Rapid Debt-Repayment Plan regardless if this is the minimum amount according to the creditors or not. Remember, they want you to pay less every month so you can keep paying forever.

This is what happens: You continue to pay the same amount each month, even as your debts go down. When you pay off one debt, you don't reduce the amount you're paying toward debt reduction—you apply what you were paying on the first debt to the next debt and so on until all debts are paid off.

Look at the Examples' Rapid Debt-Repayment Plan. This is how it works: The total of minimum monthly payments in the first month is $619. This is the amount Sam and Samantha have committed to pay every month until they are debt-free, regardless of anything their creditors say about lower payments. In Month 1, the Examples make all of the minimum monthly payments for a total of $619. In Month 2, they do the same thing. In Month 3, they make their committed payments just as they did in the past two months—except now the payment to Department Store #1 is only $12 because that is the total outstanding balance. Wow! The first zero balance. So what happens to the $23 they didn't have to send to Department Store #1 because of the zero balance? That $23 is included with the regular payment to Personal Loan (the next debt in line), increasing its payment from $108 to $131.

In Month 4, the $35 payment that used to go to Department Store #1 is now added to Personal Loan's payment so it becomes $143. This additional payment (technically prepayment of the principal) is what will get that Personal Loan paid in just seven months, including interest. The total amount paid in Month 4 is still $619 even though the number of debts has been reduced.

Now look at what happened to the Student Loan while this was going on. It reached a zero balance in Month 7 as well, so now Sam and Samantha have three debts completely paid off. But since they are committed to paying $619 every month against their debts, the payment to Visa #1 is substantially increased because the old payments for Department Store #1, Personal Loan, and Student Loan are all added to the Visa #1 payment, increasing it from $108 to $277 until it is fully paid in Month 11.

And on it goes. The Examples pay $619 every month, always taking the old payments and adding them to the payment of the next debt until they are 100 percent debt-free in Month 23!

You must agree that this is truly amazing, considering that given the slow-pay method, Sam and Samantha would have been paying on these debts for 12 or more years, provided that they never missed a payment and did not incur any new debt.

Let's Review

Here are the five steps for wiping out your debts in record time:

Step 1: You must repent. *Repent* simply means to turn around, to go in a different direction. You must repent from debting, that is, incurring new debts. If you don't complete the first step, the plan will not work.

Step 2: You must pay the same amount every month until all of your unsecured debts are paid in full. From this moment on, you must adopt the total of your current minimum monthly payments as your regular monthly obligation, not unlike your house or car payment. It will not change from month to month. It's big, it's ugly, and it's not going to disappear. Just accept it.

Step 3: List your debts in order according to the number of months left. For example, a debt to a department store of $80 total with a minimum monthly payment of $40 has about two months left (the total paid will be slightly higher than the $80 because of the interest). That one goes at the top of your list. Then if the next debt will take five months to pay off, that's listed next; then the nine-month debt, and so on.

Step 4: From here on out, ignore declining minimum monthly payments. The minimum payment in the first month of your plan is the amount you will pay until your total debt is wiped out, regardless of whether the creditor shows a lower amount due on your statement. Don't succumb to the temptation to reduce your payments as your debts are reduced.

Step 5: As one debt is paid off, apply its monthly payment to the next debt. No matter how many debts you have paid off, you must commit to pay the same total amount every month until every debt is paid.

If you want to see your Rapid Debt-Repayment Plan work even more quickly, increase your monthly commitment. Remember that the key to rapid repayment is in prepaying principal.

Take hope from these two letters from people who benefitted from the debt-reduction plan:

> I just want to say thank you—you've really opened my eyes. My Rapid Debt-Repayment Plan has me completely paid off in 36 months.
>
> I owed $14,000 in credit card debt. You're right, you get into a set pace of living the good life without realizing what you are doing to your future. In one month, I charged $1,428 in clothing on my Visa card without a second thought (at 21 percent interest!).

I got into the habit of living well when I married a man who made an incredible salary; when we divorced, it was nearly impossible to cut back. I tried to maintain the lifestyle to which I'd become accustomed. I've had to face reality, and it's been tough.

I'll be completely debt-free when I'm 34 years old, and I can't wait!

—Mary Beth

I want to let you know that I am completely debt-free! I've carried some amount of debt since I got my first credit card nearly 15 years ago. Paying the monthly bills was just a fact of life. But I followed your Rapid Debt-Repayment Plan and paid off my debts in three years. I discovered that debt doesn't *have* to be a way of life. I didn't realize the burden I was carrying until the last credit card payment was mailed off. I feel free!

I shudder to think how much money I paid in interest—in fact, it would probably make me ill to calculate how big my savings would be right now if I had all the interest money back. So I'll focus on the positive: No debt . . . and no debt *ever again*.

—Jerry

....

Chapter 8

The Principle of Preparation

How to Develop Your Freedom Account

W e are about to uncover what I am sure is a major source of your financial difficulties. I have read so many letters and talked to so many people about their financial situations that I have begun to see a pattern. To my utter amazement, the majority of these people are simply repeating what happened to me.

Most people learn to fit their regular monthly expenses into their average monthly income. In other words, there's no cushion, no fudge room. It may not be an exemplary way to handle personal finances, but it's the way most people get by. Somehow the rent gets paid, food arrives on the table, the car payment is met, and the utility companies keep providing electricity, water, and gas.

Since monthly income covers these predictable monthly payments, it is easy to get comfortable, to feel that everything is just peachy. So peachy, in fact, that it seems okay to take on a little extra debt ("it's only $15 a month, dear!") or make purchases with discretionary income (which we mistakenly define as anything that represents a balance in the checkbook). It's all right to have a few extra dinners out because there are a few extra bucks in the checking account. It's fine to splurge here and there because we seem to have enough money.

Without our noticing, monthly income and regular monthly expenses have a way of becoming dangerously close. What little cushion might have existed is eaten away by the extras. Occasional pay increases provide breathing room for a short time, but they are quickly absorbed into thin air, or so it seems.

The problem is something I call selective amnesia. It is a form of denial found far too often among those who can least afford such a malady. Let's look at the symptoms of selective amnesia and their debilitating consequences. One symptom is being totally unaware that the car, for instance, is wearing out with every mile driven. We don't come right out and say it, but we live as though the tires are going to last forever, because somehow our tires are the only ones on planet earth made of indestructible material. Each month that we do not experience flat tires or blowouts just confirms this mysterious fact. Since the car starts up every morning, doesn't leak oil, and shifts gears flawlessly month after month, we live as if it will always perform at its current level of excellence. When it comes to any kind of automobile maintenance beyond the ceremonial oil change, most people slip easily into selective amnesia.

What's more, this condition applies to far more than automobiles. Most people think the house will never need repairs, the refrigerator will never die, the hard drive will never crash, and the clothes will never wear out.

Meet the Freedom Account

Somehow you manage to pay your rent or mortgage every month because past experience has taught you that failure to do so brings swift and painful consequences. Imagine you are notified that effective immediately you will no longer pay rent (or the mortgage payment) each month but rather in one lump sum for the entire year. Your first yearly payment will be due one year from today.

Even though you aren't required to pay the rent each month, would you continue to see one-twelfth of that annual payment being as critical on a monthly basis as you now consider it? Probably not. More than likely, rent would become one of your annual expenses that you hope will somehow take care of itself when the time comes.

Knowing yourself, what do you think your chances are of coming up with the, oh, let's say $12,000 annual payment one year from now? About as good as your having cash put away for most of your other intermittent expenses! It would be natural (though not too smart) for you to feel some relief knowing you will no longer have to deal with rent on a monthly basis. Some of us would actually experience a feeling of exhilaration calculating how this new arrangement will free up an "extra" $1,000 each month. Others (those who are breaking out in a cold sweat at this very moment) know the only right way to respond is to act as if one-twelfth of the rent is still "due" every month and put that amount under the mattress or in a coffee can religiously on the first day of each month, come hell or high water. Wise people would live no differently than if the rent were due every month.

Lest any of you get too used to such an insane idea, let me bring you back to reality. Your rent or mortgage payment is due every month just as it always has been. And one-twelfth of your automobile maintenance is due every month along with one-twelfth of your property taxes and one-twelfth of quite a few things that you fail to consider on a monthly basis. Expenses that are not paid monthly are called *irregular expenses*. This is where selective amnesia becomes a virtual epidemic. When it comes to irregular expenses, many people become amnesiacs.

Talk is cheap, isn't it? And there's no place it is cheaper than when it comes to saying you're going to start planning ahead for the irregular expenses. However, I am going to teach you a method that, if followed diligently, will change your life forever. This is so exciting, so effective, so easy to handle, it borders on being miraculous. It's called (drum roll, please) the Freedom Account, and it is truly at the heart of turning your financial life around forever.

Developing a Freedom Account

The key to achieving financial ease is exerting control over your money. You can bring order and purpose to your personal finances by regularly setting aside funds in advance to cover your irregular expenses. Opening a Freedom Account will bring you a new sense of dignity, control, and personal worth. Here's how:

Step 1: Determine irregular expenses. Using last year's check registers or paid bills folder, make a list of expenses that you do not pay on a regular monthly basis. These expenses might be paid quarterly, semi-annually, or annually. Multiply to reach an annual figure and then divide by 12 so you can arrive at a figure that represents one-twelfth of the total annual expense.

Here are some fictitious and hypothetical expenses Sam and Samantha Example, our fictitious and hypothetical sample family of four, calculated to be their irregular expenses. Please don't get hung up on these dollar figures and miss the principles they represent. They are made up and do not indicate what is typical.

Auto maintenance/repairs	$900/yr divided by 12=$75/mo
Auto insurance	$540/yr divided by 12=$45/mo
Life insurance	$480/yr divided by 12=$40/mo
Property taxes	$600/yr divided by 12=$50/mo
Vacation	$900/yr divided by 12=$75/mo
Clothing	$600/yr divided by 12=$50/mo
	Total: $335/mo

Sam and Samantha receive their income monthly; therefore, they will handle their Freedom Account on a monthly basis. You may not be paid once a month; however, since it would be impossible for me to convert every illustration to fit your particular payroll schedule, I'll leave it to you to translate the principles herein to fit your particular circumstances.

Step 2: Open two checking accounts. Yes, two. Shop for a bank or credit union that offers the best terms available, such as no fee with a minimum balance, low-fee, or interest-bearing checking accounts with minimum balance. Open the two accounts at the same time and order checks for each account. (I highly recommend duplicate checks even though they cost a bit more.) Have them personalized and add the words *Regular Account* and *Freedom Account* under your name and address on the accounts and checks. If you wish to continue using your present checking account for the Regular Account, simply open a second at the same institution. The point is that you need to have two active checking accounts at a bank that will offer you the best terms and services. Do not—I repeat, do not—accept an ATM card for the Freedom Account. Having ATM access to this account will defeat its purpose.

The Regular Account will continue to accommodate your monthly expenses and typical day-to-day needs, such as groceries, gas, etc. You will continue to deposit your regular paychecks and other forms of income into this account.

Step 3: Request an automatic deposit authorization. At the time you open the accounts, request an automatic deposit authorization form (my bank calls this an Automatic Money Transfer Form), instructing the bank to transfer the monthly total of your irregular expenses ($335 is the figure Sam and Samantha will use) from your Regular Account into your Freedom Account on a specific day of the month, preferably no more than five days after the date on which you will be depositing your paycheck. Example: You are paid once a month on the 15th. You instruct the bank to automatically transfer $335 from your Regular Account into your Freedom Account on the 20th of every month. The five-day "cushion" will cover the unusual months when your regular payday falls on a holiday or weekend. The selection of your transfer date is important, because once it's established you can be sure the bank will never forget to make the transfer, nor will they be late.

Step 4: Get a loose-leaf notebook and label it "Freedom Account." As far as the bank is concerned, you have a single account that you have designated your Freedom Account. (The bank doesn't care how you refer to it; banks recognize only account numbers.) But you are going to treat it as six sub-accounts (or three or eight—whatever your particular case may be according to the number of Irregular Expenses you determined that you have; Sam and Samantha have six). In your notebook, prepare one page per sub-account similar to Sam and Samantha's Auto Maintenance/Repair Account (Figure 8.1). Keep it simple. Fill in the title, enter the amount to be deposited into that particular sub-account in the upper right-hand corner, and prepare five columns, "Date," "Transaction," "In," "Out," and "Balance," for each sub-account.

Step 5: Get in the habit. Each time you deposit your paycheck into your Regular Account, deduct the amount of your Irregular Expenses' monthly allocation ($335 for Sam and Samantha) on your Regular Account checkbook register. Don't even think about forgetting; the bank never will. It will feel weird in the beginning. You won't like making this debit entry because there are so many things you could do with the money. But you are controlling your money instead of it controlling you.

Next, go to your Freedom Account notebook and enter the individual deposits. Here is how Sam and Samantha will make their first $335 automatic transfer deposit into their Freedom Account: They will enter deposits of

$75 into Auto Maint./Repair
$45 into Auto Insurance
$40 into Life Insurance
$50 into Property Taxes
$75 into Vacation
$50 into Clothing

In the first few months of this new behavior you must not give in to the temptation of withdrawing from your Freedom Account for anything other than the purpose of the sub-account. No borrowing. Don't dip into your Life Insurance sub-account to pay your monthly utility bill—even if you promise to pay it back. You may feel coerced, you'll be tempted, you'll be afraid you can't stop yourself, but don't.

At times you will also be tempted to think of this account as a savings account, and you may find yourself skipping your true savings or even hesitating to write appropriate payments out of the Freedom Account. This is not a savings account. This money has been committed already. The account will give new meaning to the phrase *ebb and flow*. It is strictly a financial management tool.

Next month you will repeat this process. On the day you deposit your paycheck, you will go right to your Regular Account checkbook register and deduct the automatic transfer. You will then go to your Freedom Account, enter the individual deposits, and calculate the new balance for each of your sub-accounts. The total of all your sub-accounts in this second month should be two-twelfths of your annual Irregular Expenses. For Sam and Samantha, it is $670, or $335 times two.

Continue this procedure every month. In the third or fourth month, something wonderful will happen if you are diligent and don't give up. You will begin to experience a new level of comfort and tranquillity. You will feel yourself start to relax.

Here's what happened to Sam and Samantha Example shortly after they set up their Freedom Account. Sam had been trying to ignore a nagging guilt that he hadn't had the oil changed in the family car for far too long. They just didn't have the extra money, and it became something easy to ignore. Some time during month four of their new Freedom Account, it clicked in Sam's brain: Aha! Auto Maintenance!

He ran to the Freedom Account notebook and found they had a balance of $300 in the Auto Maintenance/Repair sub-account (4 months x $75 = $300). He grabbed the Freedom Account notebook and drove to the Quik Lube & Tune and asked for the $29.95 special. He entered $29.95

in the "Out" column of the Auto Maintenance/Repair sub-account page, wrote out check #101, and calculated the new balance, $270.05. He couldn't believe how good it felt. The Freedom Account had just worked.

Upon leaving work late on October 14 (two months later), Samantha was greeted by a flat tire. Rats! Just what she needed. Payday was still two weeks away, and she knew the spare was not in good shape. All the way home she "sat light" because she was so nervous about riding on the spare. And she worried about how she and Sam were committed to incurring no new debt. But she obviously had an emergency. And then it hit her. Aha! Auto Maintenance. They'd become good managers of their money, and that was exactly what they'd been preparing for! She arrived home with a smug grin on her face and scoured the newspaper to see what sales she could find on tires.

Early the following morning Sam headed for Zippee Tire Sales and purchased two new tires for $156.72. He wrote out check #102 and calculated the new balance of $263.33. It actually felt good!

Sam bounded out to the car that evening feeling quite perky with those two new paid-for tires and all, got in, turned the key. Click, click, click . . . NOTHING! Dead battery. Oh, no! First the flat tire and now this! What else could possibly go wrong? But it didn't take long for the good news to sink in. Yes! The Auto Maintenance fund!

He walked a few blocks to Sears where he found a good deal on a 48-month battery for $48.93. The Freedom Account could certainly handle the costs. He wrote check #103 to Sears for a new battery. He entered the transaction in the Freedom Account notebook on the Auto Maintenance/Repair page, calculated the new balance to be $214.40, and proceeded home, slightly ticked off but nonetheless thankful for the Freedom Account.

The following day being Saturday, Sam and Samantha decided to load the family in the car and head for the zoo. Halfway there and for absolutely no good reason, everything died—again! What was going on? The Example family was miles from a service station, and nobody in the car had any mechanical ability.

However, they simultaneously exclaimed, "Aha!" and no one came even close to the panic stage. They had no choice but to call Al's Big Tow, which charged $45 to haul them to Eddie's Electrical Shop. The kids thought it was pretty cool. Sam handed Al check #104 for $45, figured the balance to be $169.40 just in time to meet Eddie, who quickly determined that the generator was shot and needed replacement. The bad news was the cost of $143.20. The good news was they had plenty to cover the item. Samantha wrote Eddie check #105 for $143.20, calculated the new balance of $26.20, and they were on their way to the zoo.

Sam and Samantha faced four auto repair situations within a three-day period. However, they were able to keep their cool, they paid in full for each item, and what would have normally been considered crises did not derail the Examples. They had actually prepared for those kinds of inevitable repairs. In the future, as they become more comfortable with their Freedom Account, they will be able to head off these repairs by practicing *preventive* maintenance. They will begin to assess tire wear, battery life, and generator performance before the parts are completely shot. By the way, looking at the Examples' Freedom Account, you will notice Sam had a major awakening in February 1994. He figured that if he changed the oil himself, he could save money and afford to change it more often, which is probably the single most important auto maintenance activity he could perform.

He took advantage of a great sale and purchased twenty quarts of oil (check #106 for $19.54). He could no longer justify spending $29.95 to have it done when he could do it himself for less then $10 per change. In his pre-Freedom Account days, the small difference between having it done and doing it himself didn't seem to make much difference. Things really have changed for the Examples.

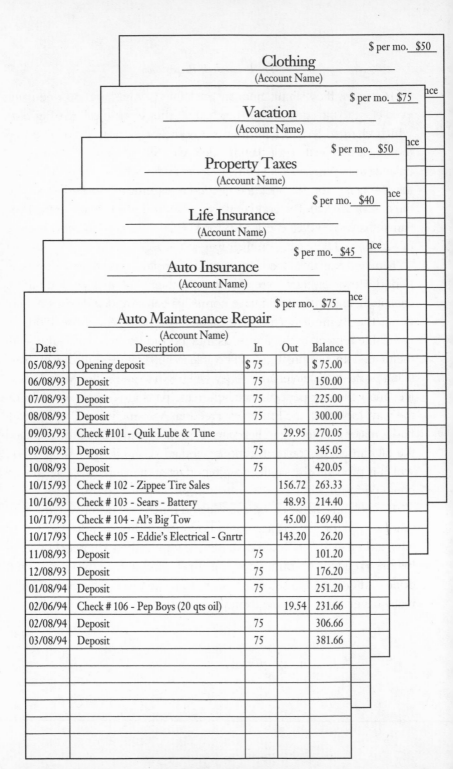

Freedom Account: Sam and Samantha Example

Clothing
(Account Name)
$ per mo. $50

Vacation
(Account Name)
$ per mo. $75

Property Taxes
(Account Name)
$ per mo. $50

Life Insurance
(Account Name)
$ per mo. $40

Auto Insurance
(Account Name)
$ per mo. $45

Auto Maintenance Repair
(Account Name)
$ per mo. $75

Date	Description	In	Out	Balance
05/08/93	Opening deposit	$ 75		$ 75.00
06/08/93	Deposit	75		150.00
07/08/93	Deposit	75		225.00
08/08/93	Deposit	75		300.00
09/03/93	Check #101 - Quik Lube & Tune		29.95	270.05
09/08/93	Deposit	75		345.05
10/08/93	Deposit	75		420.05
10/15/93	Check # 102 - Zippee Tire Sales		156.72	263.33
10/16/93	Check # 103 - Sears - Battery		48.93	214.40
10/17/93	Check # 104 - Al's Big Tow		45.00	169.40
10/17/93	Check # 105 - Eddie's Electrical - Gnrtr		143.20	26.20
11/08/93	Deposit	75		101.20
12/08/93	Deposit	75		176.20
01/08/94	Deposit	75		251.20
02/06/94	Check # 106 - Pep Boys (20 qts oil)		19.54	231.66
02/08/94	Deposit	75		306.66
03/08/94	Deposit	75		381.66

Figure 8.1

How would Sam and Samantha have handled these situations a year ago, in their pre-Freedom Account days? First of all, they would have seen each incident as a major crisis that resulted in stress, bad moods, yelling, and fretting. They would have bemoaned their bad luck and blamed the stupid car for preventing them from getting ahead. Because they wouldn't have had any more money in their Regular Account than they do now, they would've felt forced to do one of the following: Break out the plastic and hope they had enough available credit to cover the emergency; call Mom and Dad for another bail-us-out loan; write a hot check and hope the merchant doesn't call to check before they can get the heck out of there; or find some high-priced, underqualified auto repair joint that accepts their department store card. You laugh, but I think you're beginning to understand.

Other Things to Keep in Mind

A Slow and Easy Start. I suggest that in the beginning you set up your Freedom Account to handle the minimum number of *essential* irregular expenses. If you are too aggressive at first, the system will require a large monthly transfer, and depending on your cash situation, you may be setting yourself up for failure. Start out simply and then gradually ease into expanding your Freedom Account.

Other Irregular Expenses. Some items are not as predictable as auto maintenance/repair or property taxes and have a way of hitting us over the head when we can least afford them. For instance, an excellent way to keep insurance premiums low is to carry higher deductibles. But what happens if you are in an auto accident that requires you to fork over your $1,000 deductible? Ouch! That presents a huge problem for those who live paycheck to paycheck. I would advise adding a new sub-account to help with such potentially expensive emergencies.

Insurance Deductibles. This Freedom Account sub-account should grow until its balance is equal to the annual deductible of your health, home owner's, and auto deductibles. If you are nervous about raising your deductibles in the beginning, go ahead and start a sub-account, and when its balance reaches the amount equal to your current low deductibles, increase them so you will pay lower premiums. Imagine the peace of mind you will have knowing that the deductibles are there ready to be used if necessary, and if not, the account is drawing interest. That is freedom. Once your sub-account reaches the amount you determine is adequate to cover your deductibles, you as the manager of the account are free to divert future deposits into some other sub-account.

Clothing Account. You cannot imagine how many families do not list "clothing" when asked to outline their expenses. But they don't walk around naked or even wear tattered clothes. Just the opposite. I have noticed that those in the worst financial shape are often the best-dressed. Where is that money supposed to come from? Many, of course, load huge clothing expenses on credit cards or write checks using funds that were supposed to pay for groceries or utilities. With a Freedom Account, clothing becomes a legitimate monthly expense. You may want to set up a general Clothing Account for the entire family, or three separate accounts: His Clothes, Her Clothes, Kids' Clothes, or some combination thereof.

Christmas/Holiday Account. Probably nothing in the world throws more of us into a debting depression faster than approaching the month of December. Broke! And every January, you say that next year you are going to save a little bit every month for Christmas. And do you? Well, lest I sound like a broken record, your Freedom Account is the perfect way to join your own Christmas Club.

Dream Accounts. What is it that you hope to have enough money to do or be someday? Perhaps you'd like to take a class, redecorate the master bedroom, go on a special trip, start a stamp collection, or take up skiing. If you are like most of us, these things remain a dream to be fulfilled "when we get some extra money," which is never. Well, not anymore!

The Freedom Account is the way you are going to realize your dreams. Let your mind run wild. Insert new pages in your Freedom Account notebook and title them accordingly: Redecorate Master Bedroom, Room

Addition, John's Woodworking Tools, Caribbean Cruise, Sam's Dream Account, and Samantha's Dream Account. Maybe you won't be able to start funding them right now, but little by little you are going to realize your dreams, thanks to your Freedom Account.

The Freedom Account is a fabulous marriage-enhancing tool. By having their individual accounts, both partners can manage some of their own money without feeling a need to sneak around or wallow in self-pity.

Unscheduled Income. This is any money that comes into your life irregularly or unpredictably, such as rebate checks, tax refunds, freelance payments, gifts, and so on. You receive unexpected and unpredictable money all the time. It may be only a dollar here or $10 there, but what happens to it? You put it in your pocket and it is absorbed into your daily spending so fast that you hardly remember getting it. Larger amounts, such as tax refunds and consulting payments, usually go into the checking account with the intention that they will be used in some special way, but before you know it, the money is gone. And who knows where?

The Freedom Account is a wonderful solution to the case of the vanishing funds. Making a habit of depositing unscheduled income—big or small—into the Freedom Account and selecting the sub-account to which they will be credited suddenly give new meaning to surprise money. Let's say that you misjudged your federal tax withholding and end up with a refund of $1,000. If you put it into your Regular Account, it will disappear and eventually slip through your fingers via the ATM machine or some other phantom maneuver. But if you immediately put it into your Freedom Account, you will be able to decide which dream to nourish.

Common Questions About a Freedom Account

Q: Have you lost your mind? I don't have extra money every month to fund anything, let alone a Freedom Account.

A: Listen to yourself. You are acting as if maintaining your auto is optional or you can skip paying your insurance if you're a little short on cash. Do you really have a choice of whether or not to pay your property taxes or buy a few new work clothes? You are driving a car, your taxes were paid, and you dress fairly well. Exactly how did you do that? You came up with the money somehow, and you probably have a few credit card payments that help you remember the trouble you went through to do it.

The Freedom Account is not a place to squirrel away *extra* money. It is a planning device to set aside money for expenses that will inevitably arise. You will pay for these expenses one way or the other. This way, you don't constantly have to scramble and sweat to figure out how to meet the expenditures.

This step is too important to pass off as something you cannot afford. I suggest you start out with the bare minimum number of accounts, limiting them to your most essential irregular expenses. You may have to reduce your spending in other areas in order to get started with a Freedom Account, but whatever the sacrifice, no matter how painful, this is one of the nicest things you will ever do for yourself.

Q: Won't setting up a Freedom Account bring me new, unnecessary expenses, such as fees for checks and service charges?

A: Yes. However, remember that as your total balance (the balance the bank sees is the total of all of your sub-accounts) grows beyond the minimum amount required, all service fees will be waived. You will be writing very few checks from this account so check costs will be minimal. I suggest that you choose your favorite sub-account (in my case, it would be Decorating or Vacation) and designate it as the account from which you will deduct any "administrative" charges. However, this favorite account will also be credited all of the *interest* your Freedom Account will earn. If you succeed in finding a bank that pays interest on checking accounts, you are going to make some good money that will be a great bonus for your favorite sub-account. Granted, the Freedom Account balance will fluctuate over the course of a year, but you are adding to it every month; this has a positive effect on your average daily balance. In time, you will earn a nice sum of reportable interest, which should give your favorite account a boost and more than offset any costs incurred.

Q: How do I balance the Freedom Account each month?

A: Add up the current balances of the sub-accounts. They should match the bank statement's closing balance once you have made allowances for checks that haven't cleared and deposits not yet posted. Balance it just like any other checking account. If you've never done this, step-by-step instructions can be found on the back of your monthly checking account statement. Now, in the event you are at all like me and break out in a rash at the very thought of mathematical calculations, don't panic. A kind employee in the new accounts department of your bank will be more than happy to teach you this surprisingly simple process.

Q: Couldn't I create my own Freedom Account at home without opening up another checking account?

A: Sure. You could label a series of envelopes and put cash into each one every month. But problems with this approach are obvious: Because keeping large sums of cash is not smart from a security standpoint, you'd need a home safe or vault. Also, it would be too easy to engage in impulsive borrowing. If things got a little rocky, you might be tempted to skip a month or two. The Freedom Account should be a serious business activity. To make it work, you have to be committed. If you're at all like me, you need the discipline and pressure of an automatic withdrawal. It puts everything on a much more businesslike, professional level. Besides, you probably won't pay yourself interest as the bank or credit union will. Record keeping is easier, too, when you have canceled checks at tax time.

Q: What happens if my Freedom Account gets too large? Shouldn't I be investing the money?

A: Remember, this is not an investment vehicle; this is a money management tool. Most of your sub-accounts will be self-eliminating since you'll be drawing money out of them as you incur expenses. So you will never have continuously high balances. Sub-accounts such as insurance deductibles or other items that may not be self-eliminating should have a cap. For instance, your insurance deductibles may total $1,000. Once you have reached the designated amount in your Deductibles sub-account, discontinue deposits until you must make a withdrawal. If you set up the Freedom Account properly, it is not going to present you with a problem of surpluses. Besides, I would hardly call that a problem. You will be amazed at how financially functional you'll become once you have the opportunity to manage your money.

Q: In the beginning, as the sub-accounts have low balances, what will I do if I have an expense that is greater than the current balance in that sub-account?

A: Ideally, you should find a way to open each sub-account with a larger initial deposit to cover this situation. Example: You open your Freedom Account on October 1. Your semiannual property tax bill is due on December 10. If your monthly property tax deposit into the Freedom Account is $75, you will not have the $450 necessary to make the payment. You will have contributed only $225 total (3 x $75) into that particular sub-account. You should make an initial deposit into the sub-account to jump-start the process. By contributing an additional $225 into the account on October 1 to anticipate the shortfall, the problem would be solved. As you set up the Freedom Account, you might see where a few hours of overtime or a moonlighting position for a few weeks would raise the funds necessary to launch your Freedom Account in such a way that you'll be fully prepared for the first expense. However, even if you can't manage the additional funding in the first month, don't let this become an excuse not to get started.

Let's look at another scenario. Say you have a $75 balance in your Auto Maintenance sub-account and you incur a $150 repair item during the first month. What do you do? Write a check out of your Freedom Account for the $75, and supplement the balance from your Regular Account. Do not borrow from other Freedom sub-accounts. While it pains me to suggest it, if you have absolutely no other way to come up with $75 (try hard—I mean *really* hard), I feel it would be better this one last time to put the balance on a credit card and then pay the credit card payment from the Auto Maintenance sub-account. I recommend this only if the borrowed funds can be repaid within the following 30 days.

Example: Your Auto Maintenance/Repair sub-account has a balance of $75. Your repair bill is $150. You write a check for the $75 from the Freedom Account and pay for the balance with your credit card. By the time the bill comes, you will have made another $75 deposit into the Auto Maintenance/Repair sub-account, allowing you to write a check from the Freedom Account to pay off the credit card in full without incurring an interest charge. Going through these steps of depositing into the Freedom Account and writing a check to cover the $75 credit card bill is necessary in order to keep everything straight and your sub-account page correct.

Accept the fact that it will take a little time to get the Freedom Account working smoothly. But don't let a little rough water in the beginning convince you to abandon such a wonderful, life-changing tool.

Chapter 9

The Principle of Restraint

How to Live Within Your Means

It's time to start drawing your monthly financial blueprint. I prefer not to think of this as preparing a budget. Quite frankly, to me the word *budget* sounds confining and depriving (kind of like *straitjacket* and *diet*). Instead, we're going to develop a *plan*.

Think about it: Great things are done with plans. Battles are won, houses are built, gold medals are won. So rather than force you to wriggle into something that is about as well-suited to you as another person's prescription eyeglasses, I'm going to help you design your own custom Monthly Spending Plan.

Remember in chapter 4 you started a new habit of keeping Daily and Weekly Spending Records? Now is the time to pull them out. You'll need them to create a Monthly Spending Record, which will lead into the ultimate Money Makeover tool—the Monthly Spending Plan.

So far we have determined that the key to balancing your finances is to start giving, start saving, stop the debt spiral by repaying debts quickly, and prepare for irregular expenses with a Freedom Account. Now you need to take control of the day-by-day spending that seems so out of whack.

You will need a few tools in order to get started: a pencil, pad of paper, and calculator. If you want to get really fancy, you can pick up a ledger or budget book at an office supply store or dust off that financial software or spreadsheet program you bought for your personal computer. Any of these things will work just fine to assist in drawing up this blueprint.

Step 1: Determine Your Average Monthly Income.

Regardless of your payroll schedule or the frequency with which you receive other sources of income, you must come up with your average monthly income, the number that when multiplied by 12 equals your annual gross income. You will be working with gross—that is, before tax—figures.

Note: If you are self-employed as an entrepreneur or commissioned salesperson, don't think this chapter cannot apply to you. However, you may wish to jump ahead to chapter 11 to learn how to determine your average monthly income before going farther in this chapter.

When coming up with this income figure, include all sources of income, such as salary, wages, dividend and interest income, child support payments, alimony, and so on, using before-tax figures. It's income if you get this money on a regular basis, can predict its arrival, and can spend it.

Here's a quick formula to determine your average monthly income if you receive it other than once a month:

Weekly: Multiply your weekly income by 4.333
Biweekly: Multiply your biweekly income by 2.167
Semimonthly: Multiply your semimonthly income by 2

Quarterly: Divide your quarterly income by 3
Annually: Divide your annual income by 12

Why should you use pretax income figures? Because everything withheld from your taxes represents "expenses" that you are obligated to pay, even though some of the deductions may well be savings or retirement plans. These are expenses just like your rent and groceries, and it is important that you begin to recognize them as such. Your health insurance premiums and all of the other amounts that keep showing up as deductions on your pay stub are expenses you pay. Some of the deductions may be optional, meaning you have the ability to eliminate or change them, but they're still expenses.

Back to your income. Once you have come up with your accurate average monthly income figure, write down that number. We'll be using it later.

Step 2: Make a List of Your Expense Categories.

You have fixed expenses (car payment, rent, mortgage payment, etc.) and flexible expenses (food, gasoline, telephone, utilities, etc.). Refer to the List of Possible Expenses on pages 100-102 to help you remember all of the ways that you spend money. This is an exhaustive list of every type of expense I could think of divided into main categories and subcategories. Just pick out the ones that apply to you. You might want to use the main categories (Housing, Transportation, etc.), or you might want to go into more detail. You can combine categories or add new ones. The point is that your list of Expense Categories should be unique to you and your family. Do not repeat any of the categories that have already been listed in your Freedom Account Notebook or Rapid Debt-Repayment Plan. Instead, list Freedom Account as one category and Rapid Debt-Repayment Plan as another. Be sure to include categories for Savings and Giving.

Try to be neither too detailed nor too general. Too many categories will be unmanageable. Too few categories will give you only a vague idea of where you are. I recommend the average family should have 10 to 20 categories on their Monthly Spending Plan, including the four mandatory categories of Savings, Giving, Freedom Account, and Rapid Debt-Repayment

Plan. Don't forget to include categories for federal and state tax withholding, Social Security, and other payroll deductions. These are major
expenses that we often fail to take into consideration when looking at our
total financial picture. I suggest you have one category for Taxes (state,
federal, and Social Security, which is also referred to as FICA) and then
another category, Other Withholding, to handle everything else.

To make sure you haven't forgotten anything, take a look through your
checkbook register, payroll stubs, and paid bills folder to see how you
spent your money in the last two or three months. Take note of your ATM
withdrawals. (Have any idea where that money went?) This whole exercise
should help you come up with an idea of your typical monthly expenses.

Step 3: Draft Your Monthly Spending Plan.

Get a sheet of paper and make up a form using Figure 9.1 as your
guide. Transfer your Expense Categories to the Monthly Spending Plan
form. Using the past as an indicator, fill in the "Plan" column across from
each category with the dollar amount you plan to spend in each category
during the next month. The "E/O" column is where you will honestly indicate whether this expense is "essential" or "optional." Make sure you have
not combined any essential expenses with optional ones when you made
up your category list. You may need to do some real soul-searching when
you make this determination for each entry. For example, I know you
probably prefer to think of cable TV and your cellular phone as essential
expenses. Trust me, they aren't. Mark them "O."

When you have finished filling in an amount for each category, calculate and enter the total of your planned spending. Now fill in your average
monthly income. Take a deep breath, go get a glass of water, and compare
the two figures ("Plan" column total and Average Monthly Income).

If your planned spending is more than your income, perhaps we have
begun to uncover the root of your financial problems. If your "Plan"
column came in less than your income, go on to the next step. If not, now
is the time to decide what you are going to do about this situation. You
cannot go on spending more money than you have each month.

Since you have determined to stop relying on credit to cover your regular expenses, and allowing your bills to become delinquent is no longer an option, you must find ways to reduce your regular monthly expenses.

Go back over each category, one by one. You may need to eliminate some of your optional entries for a while. Small sacrifices will reward you well in the future. You know you cannot mess with the Freedom Account (unless, of course, you have included sub-accounts that represent optional spending and could be eliminated for the time being) or your Rapid Debt-Repayment Plan. Your new commitment to these areas of planning ahead and paying off debt is absolutely essential to your Money Makeover. You will probably need to redraw this initial Monthly Spending Plan many times until you get it just right.

Sometime before the first day of the month for which you have designed this Monthly Spending Plan, you should have things organized. Let me assure you that your plan will be in a constant state of change, so don't feel defeated if you don't get it exactly right in the first few months.

Step 4: Activate Your Monthly Spending Plan.

From now on, you will look at each month as having four weeks regardless of what day of the week the first falls on or how many total days are in the month: Days 1–7 will always be Week 1; Days 8–14 will be Week 2; Days 15–21 will be Week 3; Days 22 through the end of month will be Week 4. It doesn't matter that the fourth week of every month will have anywhere from six to nine days.

Step 5: Count and Record.

One of your new mandatory behaviors has to do with counting and recording. As the month begins, it is necessary that you and anyone else who spends the family's income agree to keep a written notation of how the money is spent. Not difficult, but extremely necessary. Every expenditure, no matter how small, must be accounted for and recorded from now on. Here's how you will do it: As you spend during the week, write down two things: "How much?" and "What for?" Every time you spend cash or write a check, you must record it. At the end of each week, tally up all expenditures for the week and record these totals by category in the appropriate "week" column on your Monthly Spending Plan. You may find yourself reworking your categories when, for example, you can't figure out in which category to record "Newspaper—35¢."

Step 6: Face the Month-End Truth.

On the last day of the month (which will always be the last day of Week 4), fill in the last column, "Wk 4," with your expenses from Week 4. Run individual category totals across and enter the amounts in the "Actual" column. Did you go over or under your "Plan" amount in each category? Enter the difference in the "+/-" column.

Now total the "Actual" column, adding up what you actually spent in all categories. How does this compare with your "Plan" column?

Let me predict what happened during the first month: (1) You had expenditures for which you had prepared no categories; and (2) You spent far more than you had planned and found yourself hopelessly broke and dying to write a bad check in Week 4. Failure to acknowledge your true expenses is the reason you have lost control of your finances. You didn't mean to overspend—you were simply unaware of your true expenses! I hope you have a lot more insight now than you had a month ago.

Here's the beautiful thing about a Monthly Spending Plan: You are in charge! As a good manager, you need to start planning immediately for next month.

Step 7: Rethink Optionals.

A logical place to cut expenses is in the area of nonessential items. Perhaps canceling cable TV or mowing the yard yourself might be in order for a while to reduce expenses. Maybe you've been indulging in luxuries that you really cannot afford at this time. (Chapter 10, "Cheap Shots," contains many ideas for cutting expenses.)

Step 8: Prepare Next Month's Spending Plan.

This is going to be easy because you have all the figures from last month. As you fill in the "Plan" column, use the data from last month's

"Actual" column to give you a starting point. Look at your flexible categories, such as Food or Utilities. How much could you reasonably reduce
these items in the coming month? How much do you need to reduce
spending in this area next month in order to come in under plan? Plug in
a figure, and then do everything you can to reach the goal.

A Monthly Spending Plan is absolutely mandatory if you want to
achieve financial independence. It doesn't take time; it *saves* time. It
doesn't prevent you from having the desires of your heart; it takes you
from dreams to reality.

Living with a Monthly Spending Plan

From now on, you will have two basic financial tools—your checkbook and your Monthly Spending Plan. This is where it gets a little tricky,
but as long as you understand the function of each, you should not have
a problem.

You must live according to your Monthly Spending Plan. For instance,
perhaps you have designated $200 as your planned spending in the category
of Groceries for the month. You need to spend no more than $200, just as
the plan states. However, your cash flow may ebb and flow through the
month, and if you have a current balance of $4.32 in your Regular Account,
you'd best not run out and purchase $200 in groceries simply because that
is the amount you have allotted on your Monthly Spending Plan!

You have based your Monthly Spending Plan on your *average monthly
income*. Because your paycheck and other sources of income may not arrive
on time, you may need to adjust and fine-tune the timing of your spending
to accommodate your "cash flow." There will be times when you need to
delay expenditures so that you do not move ahead of your deposits.

On the other hand, there will be months when your actual income is
significantly greater than your monthly planned spending. This is where
you will need all of the discipline and restraint you can muster. Your
common sense will tell you that the balance in the checkbook is not some
newfound windfall. While I know that a balance of any significance in
your Regular Checking Account may not be something you're familiar

with, get familiar with it. If you work your Money Makeover right, this will happen, so keep your hands off it! Your *average monthly income* has not changed; don't live as though it has.

You remember figuring "averages" in math class, don't you? You added up a list of numbers; some were small, others were large, but when you added them up and divided by the total number of entries in your list, you ended up with the average.

The same principle is true of your income. Some months your actual income will be one of the smaller numbers in the list; other months it will be a larger one. But if you spend the excess or the amount over the average because you see a balance in the checking account, you are going to be in big trouble next month or the next. For example, let's suppose you make $36,000 a year and you're paid every other week. Your average monthly income is $3,000, but 10 months a year you'll get two paychecks totaling $2,769.23 and two months a year you'll get three checks totaling $4,153.85.

Perhaps it's time for you to force a little financial maturity upon yourself. It's okay to have a balance in your checking account. It will not burn a hole there—just don't touch it. Allow your Money Makeover plan to work. Believe me, it will all come out right by the end of the year if you will be patient, diligent, persistent, and disciplined.

I encourage you to take the simple Monthly Spending Plan and expand or enhance it so that your makeover becomes uniquely yours. I don't know what will work for you on a day-to-day basis. Perhaps you will want to use envelopes or coffee cans to keep your spending straight. I don't want to tell you how often to go to the grocery store. I do know what works for me, but it may not work for you. (We grocery shop once a month, buy in bulk—and make it last. There have been times we've shopped for two months, which presents a whole new twist when living by a Monthly Spending Plan.)

Optimize your growth by consciously focusing on restraint. Lack of restraint has caused you to make some foolish purchases in the past for which you may still be paying. Restraint is good, because it allows you to bring into action all of your intelligence and reason (which were probably ignored when you lived impulsively and made off-the-cuff financial decisions).

On the following page you will find a hypothetical Monthly Spending Plan for our friends, Sam and Samantha Example. Remember, this is hypothetical and in no way suggests a perfect scenario. Use it as an example for creating your own plan.

MONTHLY SPENDING PLAN
Month of August 1996

Category	Wk 1	Wk 2	Wk 3	Wk 4	Actual $ Spent in Mo.	Plan $ to Spend	Amt. $ +/-	E/O
Savings	100		100		200	200	-	E
Giving	100		100		200	200	-	E
Freedom Account	335				335	335	-	E
Rapid Debt-Repymt Pln	619				619	619	-	E
Mortgage Payment			850		850	850	-	E
Car Payment		172			172	172	-	E
Gasoline	18	21	16	15	70	80	-10	E
Groceries	70	72	78	65	285	300	-15	E
Food (out)	35	27	14	40	116	75	+41	O
Utilities			155		155	180	-25	E
Telephone				24	24	37	-13	E
Fed & State Taxes	816				816	816	-	E
Other Withholding	256				256	256	-	E
Baby-sitter	10			10	20	25	-5	O
Kids' Allowance		20			20	20	-	O
Newspaper/Magazines	3	5	6	2	16	20	-4	O
TOTALS	2362	317	1319	156	4154	4170	-16	

Figure 9.1

Average Monthly Income $ 4,583.00
Total Actual $ Spent This Month: $ - 4,154.00
Underspent or <Overspent> $ 429.00 (underspent)

If overspent $_____ Income $_____ = _____% reduction
required for next month

You will notice that the Examples' savings and giving amount to about
5 percent of their gross income. While not optimum, this is a healthy start.
Please keep in mind that the Giving category reflects only cash contributions and does not reflect nonmonetary gifts of time or talent.

You may be curious as to why the Examples have so few categories on
their plan. This is the beautiful thing about having a Freedom Account and
a Rapid Debt-Repayment Plan. None of the categories covered there needs
to be repeated. The simple entries Freedom Account and Rapid Debt-
Repayment Plan take care of it. Categories such as clothing, entertainment,
medical/dental, etc., would not show up individually on the Monthly
Spending Plan, but would be handled in the Freedom Account.

Notice that the Examples underspent by $429 in the month of August
1996. They are living beneath their means. I would recommend that they
leave this balance in their Regular Account as a cushion. Eventually, if this
excess continues on a regular basis, they should increase their savings allotment and devote the rest to their Rapid Debt-Repayment amount.

Two years from now when they have completed their Rapid Debt-
Repayment Plan, the Examples will immediately have $619 "extra" each
month. What should they do? Wow! Their choices are many.

They could open a New Car sub-account in their Freedom Account and
fund it to the tune of $619 each month; they could split that amount
between several existing Freedom Account sub-accounts; or they could
start prepaying their mortgage by that amount each month. They could
expect to pay off their home mortgage in record time with that kind of
healthy prepayment of principal.

Options. The wise management of our money gives us wonderful
options, and that's what a Money Makeover is all about!

List of Possible Expenses

Giving
   Church/synagogue
   Charities

Savings
   Investment
   College
   Retirement
   Other

Freedom Account

Rapid Debt-Repayment Plan

Housing
   Mortgage payment
   Rent

Home Maintenance
   Maintenance
   Grounds care
   Other

Utilities
   Electricity
   Water
   Gas
   Heating oil
   Telephone
   Cable TV
   Trash pickup

Food
   Groceries
   Business lunches
   Fast food
   Restaurants
   School lunches
   Other

Clothing
   Adult
   Children
   Laundry
   Dry cleaning
   Other

Medical
   Medicine/drugs
   Dental
   Eyeglasses
   Doctor and dentist visits
   Medical insurance
   Dental insurance
   Hospital costs
   Other

Transportation
  Licensing/registration
  Gasoline
  Oil/antifreeze
  Tires
  Repairs
  Inspection
  Parking
  Public transportation
  Other

Personal/Household
  Furniture
  Kitchen appliances
  Utility appliances
  Electronic appliances
  Linens
  Utensils
  Tools
  Beauty shop and supplies
  Barber shop and supplies
  Fitness center
  Toiletries
  Reading material
  Pets and supplies
  Veterinarian

Insurance
  Auto
  Life
  Property-casualty
  Renter
  Other

Gifts
  Birthdays
  Anniversaries
  Business-related
  Wedding/baby
  Christmas/holiday
  Other

Recreation/Entertainment
  Vacations
  Shows/movies
  Sporting events
  Dining Clubs/parties
  Hobbies
  Other

Taxes (Withheld)
  Income (Federal)
  Income (State)
  Social Security (FICA)
  Other

Other Payroll Withholding
  Health insurance
  Disability
  Unemployment insurance

Miscellaneous
  Tuition
  School supplies
  School room and board
  Athletic fees
  Union dues
  Professional fees
  Licenses
  Lessons
  Other

Support/Child Care
  Alimony
  Child support
  Day care
  Baby-sitting
  Support of parents
  Children's allowances
  Other

How to Live Within Your Means

If your efforts to design a Monthly Spending Plan that fits within your income have left you with a three-alarm headache and a feeling of defeat, take heart. You are not alone, and there are remedies. If you are determined, nothing can stop you. But there are no instant solutions. This process takes time. You must never give up. In time you will be able to look back in amazement to see that by taking one step at a time, you were able to completely change the direction of your life.

There are only three ways you can change the numbers on your Monthly Spending Plan:

1. Increase your income.
2. Sell your assets.
3. Decrease your expenses.

1. Increasing income. This is probably the first thing most of us consider when facing financial hardship because it appears to be the quickest and most painless solution. However, of the three remedies listed above, I believe this is the least desirable. Increasing income does nothing to address the root problem of habitual overspending and poor money management. More money just provides more opportunity and greater ability to overspend, and allows the debt-prone individual to qualify for more debt. Increasing income invariably increases expenses in the form of taxes, child care, transportation, clothing, and meals out. It takes a great deal of additional income to realize a substantial net effect after all the tax collectors have taken their share.

Consider the effect that increasing your income has had in the past. Think back five years. You have increased your income since then, so why wasn't that the solution?

2. Selling assets. This is an excellent way to make a one-time or occasional adjustment in your Monthly Spending Plan, provided you have assets with a resale value. The best way to find out if you do is to make a list of everything you own. Take each item and assign it a market value, the amount you could reasonably sell it for within the next 90 days. (This is not a bad exercise to go through once a year, even if you have no intention of selling anything.)

Next, go through your list and rate each item according to these criteria:

Things I don't want to keep

Things I could live without

Things I can't live without

You might be amazed at the total market value of all the stuff cluttering up your home and your life that you could easily live without. Every day people just like you are getting extra cash by selling things they no longer use or need. I suggest you cautiously decide what you have that you can actually live without. Don't make hasty decisions or you may live to regret selling something you still need.

Holding a garage sale is an excellent way to liquidate low-priced goods. For more valuable things, consult with an antique dealer or consignment store owner. Perhaps your area has an auction that accepts the kinds of items you wish to sell. Look through your local classified ads to see what price others are asking for similar goods. Study the ads to see which ones are the most appealing. Let your friends and neighbors know of anything you have for sale. Your best customer might be right under your nose.

Money realized from selling assets can be used in several ways: to speed up the Rapid Debt-Repayment Plan; to increase the monthly income in the month in which the transaction takes place; or to deposit the funds in one or more sub-accounts of your Freedom Account, thereby reducing the monthly withdrawal from your Regular Account.

Selling assets is a good way to raise your income, but not many of us can count on hosting a successful garage sale more than once a year or so. However, by using the proceeds to pay down debt, the net effect on your bottom line will be permanent. If you apply the proceeds to meet your regular monthly expenses, the result will have an effect only in that month.

3. Decreasing expenses. Cutting expenses is by far the most desirable way to live within your means. Example: If you work overtime in order to earn an additional $100, you will be lucky to see $50 that you can apply to your Monthly Spending Plan. However, if you cut $100 from your monthly food bill, you will instantly see a $100 net effect on your Monthly Spending Plan's bottom line month after month.

Decreasing expenses has many other benefits that make this by far the quickest and best way to get your income and your expenses in line. By forcing you to pay attention to what you are spending and finding ways to spend less, you'll increase your consciousness about spending, you'll become a better steward of what you have, and you will be better able to see which things in life really matter. You'll become more appreciative by waiting until you can purchase something with cash. You'll find yourself more flexible, and you'll travel through life with a spring in your step rather than a pain in your neck!

The idea of reducing your living expenses to 80 percent of your income might seem impossible right now. But it's not. We humans are amazing creatures. How few our true needs, how vast our wants! The trick to achieving this reducing act is in assessing your present situation, deciding what percentage of reduction must take place, and then proceeding to work on every area accordingly. It can be done. You have a new mission in life: Save money any way you can!

There are literally thousands of ways to cut your expenses. However, until you have a plan and a way to measure the effect of cutting expenses, it seems meaningless to save a dollar here when you are in a major financial crunch. To be honest, it seems as frustrating as trying to drain the ocean cup by cup. This kind of frustration may prevent you from making any change in your spending habits. But when you have a clear-cut Monthly Spending Plan, these savings multiplied over and over will make the unbelievable possible.

Four Tricks of the Trade

1. Ask yourself tough questions. Because you are going to become increasingly conscious of every penny you spend (you will be writing it down), you can train yourself to approach spending in a new way. From now on, before you make a significant purchase (you decide what *significant* is—perhaps anything over $20), stop and ask yourself these questions:

Do I really need this? If the answer is yes, go on. If the answer is no, bravo! You just saved yourself from a stupid purchase.

Do I already have something that would do just as well? If the answer is yes, you've just saved yourself money. If the answer is no, go on.

Could I find a cheaper substitute? If the answer is yes, don't buy now. If the answer is no, go on.

If after applying this little test you find you still need it, you don't have anything else that would do just as well, and you need all the quality you can afford, go ahead and make your selection. And then? *Wait* for a full 24 hours—a full week is far more desirable—until you actually make the purchase. End result? If you go through with the transaction (and you won't believe how many times you'll change your mind during the mandatory waiting period), you will never wonder if it was the right thing to do.

2. As much as possible, live with cash. When I refer to *cash,* I mean full payment up front—no credit cards, no bad checks, no games, no manipulation.

For a long time, the only way I could guarantee that kind of honest transaction was to pay for everything with cash. I was too crazy with a checkbook, and credit cards were out of the question. I have, however, become quite responsible with a business checking account over the past few years and can even be trusted with our personal checkbook. I haven't bounced a check in nearly 14 years! In some ways, I have become obsessive about not messing up by balancing on a daily basis. It works for me, so that's what I do. But for day-to-day, nonbusiness purchases, I use cash. I haven't been mugged and don't even worry about it because I carry so little cash at any one time.

I recommend that anyone with an overspending problem chuck the checkbook and credit cards and depend on cash and/or money orders. This will put the brakes on the insanity of spending money you don't have. And my experience is that if you force yourself to live with cash, you will spend less because it forces you to be a much more careful consumer. Try it the next time you go to the grocery store. Leave the checkbook at home and take just the amount of money you have allotted for groceries.

3. Never buy better quality than you need. For example, if you need something for a single use, you might be wise to buy the cheapest thing you can find or rent it. But when it comes to something like a mattress, which you want to last for many years and consistently give you a great night's rest, you would be well-advised to buy the highest quality you can possibly afford . . . with cash.

4. Never buy new until you have considered used. The secondary market in this country for everything from automobiles to zithers is absolutely astounding. I'm not saying you should *never* buy anything new; just consider buying used before possibly paying five to 10 times as much for new. You're going to love what that kind of transaction does for your Monthly Spending.Plan.

The wonderful thing about living within your means is that as you practice saving and giving, as you assess your true needs and put your wants and desires into proper perspective, and as you plan for the future, your anxiety level diminishes and abundance begins to flow—abundance in the form of contentment and joy as well as money and material things. The balance is rewarded. I can't explain it. I just accept it. Joyfully!

As Your Means Change

Now is the time to determine how you will handle increases or decreases in future income. Failure to plan for such occurrences happened to you in the past. As your income increased, you hardly noticed it because of all the overspending you were doing. When it decreased, the bottom fell out of your world.

Using Sam and Samantha as an example, let's say that Sam receives a 10 percent salary increase on January 1. If they have not planned ahead for such an occurrence, it is likely the Examples could head into the new year with a false sense of having $5,000 extra to *spend*. And what about the new income Samantha will be generating from her home-based desktop publishing business? Without the security of knowing exactly how to handle these increases in their income, they could easily be deceived to believe they can go out and buy all kinds of neat stuff. On the other hand, what if Sam gets laid off and has a 90-day period of unemployment?

I know this is going to sound like an old broken record, but you must start with step one and go right on through. And step one was? Determine your Average Monthly Income. So back to the planning board you go, adjusting figures so that you come up with your new Average Monthly Income.

Next, you must go to your Monthly Spending Plan and start adjusting. Savings need to be increased or decreased to reflect the new income base. Giving must be adjusted. Taxes and Other Withholding must be adjusted to account for the increased income or lack thereof.

Once these adjustments are made, leave your spending plan alone for the time being if the adjustment is caused by an increase in income. Give your new situation three or four months to settle in. If you see that you are consistently spending well under your income, readjust.

Perhaps now would be the time to increase your entertainment allotment, increase your deposits, add new sub-accounts to the Freedom Account, or boost your Rapid Debt-Repayment monthly allotment. The key is that as your income increases, you respond cautiously and slowly. Don't blow it by jumping into outrageous new debt.

Eventually, as an experienced financial manager, you will know when you're ready to take on a larger mortgage or higher rent. You'll know when it's the right time to buy another car (with cash) or take the cruise you've been dreaming about.

And if the adjustment is due to a *decrease* in income? Then you need to go right down the list and adjust the figures according to the percentage drop in income. It could be a bleak picture, or if you have been diligent in paying off debt, you might be pleasantly surprised at how flexible you have become.

The key is finding balance and planning ahead. Determine ahead of time exactly how and what you will adjust if and when your income changes. It may well go up, and then on the other hand, it could go down. The steps in adjusting your Monthly Spending Plan will remain the same.

Chapter 10

....

Cheap Shots

Hundreds of Ways to Cut Expenses

I n your lifetime, you and your family will probably purchase an entire fleet of cars, thousands of items of clothing, tons of groceries, and numerous insurance policies. You will drive millions of miles, repair and replace many major appliances, eat thousands of restaurant meals, and help keep several utility companies in business. With a little planning and a lot of determination, there is no reason you should pay full price for any of these goods and services.

Now that you are committed to living well on 80 percent of your income, it is critical that you s-t-r-e-t-c-h every dollar to its absolute maximum, and there's no better time than right now to get started. Besides, when you learn to scrimp on unimportant areas of your life, you can splurge where it counts. You can't begin too soon to reduce your expenses and improve your life.

Food

Never shop when hungry. Your hunger will override your good intentions every time!

Stick to a list prepared ahead of time. A little discipline never hurt anyone.

Learn to cook and bake from scratch. Get out your cookbooks and be brave. You'll save a lot of money, you'll eat more nutritiously, and you might just enjoy it. Come on—if I can do it, anyone can!

Shop with cash. You will be a much more careful shopper knowing that if you go over your limit without a checkbook or credit card to fall back on, you will be embarrassed at the checkout counter.

Use coupons carefully. Very carefully! Some slick marketing program is hoping against hope that you will clip and cash in. Use coupons only for items you would normally buy even if you didn't have the coupon and only if it is truly a savings. Check other brands that might be on sale or are already cheaper. Manufacturers often offer coupons as incentives on new products or luxury treats. But you're not saving anything if you're suckered into it.

If you do have a qualified coupon, buy the smallest size allowable. You'll usually save a higher percentage of the purchase price by buying the smallest size.

Find a market that will double the coupon's value. This practice varies throughout the country, but if you do have good coupons, make sure you find a way to double them. Some stores even triple them on certain days.

Shop less frequently. You will be forced to make the food last longer, and you will become more creative. Start by doubling the time between trips. If you go to the market every day, stretch it to every other day. Once a week? Shop for two weeks next time. You'll waste less, use less, and spend proportionately less.

Don't shop at convenience or specialty stores. You won't find any bargains there. Specialty items are expensive, and you can find quality substitutes at your regular or discount supermarket.

Stretch fruit juice. Mix 50/50 with generic brand club soda or seltzer.

Drink water. Your doctor will love you and so will your food bill. Keep a pitcher of chilled water in the fridge. Rave about its wonderful qualities to your young children. They'll think it's a treat if you are convincing enough.

Find a thrift bakery outlet. These stores generally have fresh products (not necessarily day-old) at cut-rate prices. Shop on special 10 percent off days. Load up the freezer.

Make your own substitutes. Instead of buying mixes and ready-to-go cooking products—for muffins and cakes, biscuits and rolls, hot chocolate, and so on—watch for recipes and make your own.

Eliminate choices at meals. Stick to your plan and let your family know that from now on there will be only two choices: take it or leave it.

Leave the kids home when you shop. You will stick to your shopping list with much less frustration and stress if you fly solo.

Stick to the perimeter of your supermarket. That is where you will typically find the produce, meat, and dairy products. The center aisles are the prepackaged and preprocessed high-priced items, aka the danger zone. Refuse to tread where you don't have to.

Buy the largest quantity rather than individual portions. Take soda pop, for instance. Cans usually cost more than bottles for some reason (unless you are using a coupon, in which case you have already learned to buy the smallest size allowable).

If your market charges for grocery bags, bring your own. Recycling is a pretty good habit to develop.

Change eating habits. Learn about the nutritious benefits of beans and rice instead of meat. Sneak in vegetarian meals. Experiment with legumes and grains—they are much cheaper and quite good.

Come up with creative menu titles for what otherwise might be considered plain and boring. Add your ideas to these suggestions: Baked Potato Bar; Chef Salad Night; Bits and Pieces (my kids' favorite meal when they were little, this is any combination of things in the fridge cut up to bite-size and cleverly arranged on a plate); Smorgasbord Night (a glorious array of this and that—leftovers that you couldn't even think of throwing away); Hors d'oeuvres and Mocktails.

Shop at a discount warehouse store. You'll give up the glitzy ambiance, but you'll save big! (Caution: Some have annual membership fees, so weigh the benefits.)

Learn to s-t-r-e-t-c-h. Oatmeal or bread crumbs stretch a pound of ground beef into a pound and a half or more; nonfat dry milk stretches a gallon of milk into two; borax and baking soda stretch automatic dishwashing detergent. The possibilities are endless.

Create cheap gourmet coffee. Break up a cinnamon stick into dry coffee grounds or add a few drops of vanilla extract to brewed coffee.

Buy in bulk. This will cut down your trips to the grocery store and will often save 50 percent of the unit cost. Reorganize your kitchen and pantry. Find places outside the kitchen to store dry and canned goods. Repackage large amounts into small units.

Become a shelf-life expert. Buying in bulk will do you no good if you end up throwing most of it away due to spoilage. Some things last indefinitely, while others spoil, even if frozen, after a certain period of time.

Use cloth napkins. Fine restaurants do. Make your own from sheets or other soft fabric. Just think of all the disposable products you could do without (paper plates, paper napkins, Styrofoam cups, plastic cutlery, paper towels).

Consider generic and store brands. Some generic items are awful and others are exactly the same product as the name brand alternative. Do some experimenting, especially if your store offers "satisfaction guaranteed." If you don't like it, the store may let you exchange it.

Make eating at home fun. Rearrange your eating area. Make a new tablecloth. Use place mats. Play background music. Light some candles. Have a picnic in the family room.

Plant a garden. You don't need major acreage to grow tomatoes, herbs, and an occasional row of lettuce. Consider the square-foot method or container gardening (go to your library for a how-to book).

Keep a price book. Start keeping a notebook that lists the prices of regularly purchased items at various stores. Refer to it when you see specials or ads to determine whether you're really getting a bargain.

Check the reduced and day-old sections of the store. But be sure to check the expiration dates. No buy is a good buy if you have to throw it out.

Avoid shopping on the first of the month. Some stores have been known to raise their prices during the time welfare and Social Security checks come out.

Shop during mark-down time. Ask the butcher or produce person when they mark down items. You'll be surprised how helpful they can be, and you'll get the best of the sale items.

Don't shop when you are exhausted. You will not be as disciplined or effective.

Watch for refunds and rebates. Be careful. Your time is precious, but if you can fit it in, there's money to be made.

Make your own pizza stone. This is the key to professional-quality pizza. Instead of paying $30 for a commercial pizza stone, pick up an unglazed terra-cotta tile at your local hardware for about a buck. Place on lowest rack in oven, heat up to 400 degrees, and bake pizza directly on tile.

Always use powdered dry milk for baking. If a recipe calls for cream or condensed milk, use only half the usual amount of water you would use with the dry milk.

Use paper coffee filters several times. Just carefully rinse them off between using.

Make your own salad dressings and croutons. You will save at least 50 percent.

Reserve eating out for special occasions. Restaurant and fast food will cost you at least double. Consider eating out an occasional treat.

Weigh all produce, even if it is priced per item. You won't believe the difference in weight of the prebagged carrots, for instance! Even with a weight printed on the bag, the real weight may be quite different. Heads of lettuce priced individually can differ in weight by as much as half a pound! Get the most for your money.

Go to a farmers' market. You can buy fresh fruit and vegetables at great prices. Some cities hold these markets only in the warm months; in other areas, they're held year-round.

Buy produce in a bag for the best value. Watch out: Often the bruised and spoiled fruit will find its way into the bottom of a bag. So pick out the best bag.

Load up on loss leaders. These are the advertised sale items that the store uses as bait to get you in the door. Buy as much as you can reasonably use and will still fit into your spending plan.

Store cartons of cottage cheese and sour cream upside down in fridge. They will keep twice as long.

Cook in cast-iron pots. Doing this boosts the iron content of food. Soup simmered for a few hours in an iron pot has almost 30 times more iron than soup cooked in another pan. Health is important in keeping down medical expenses.

Keep fish fresh and odorless. Here's how: Rinse with fresh lemon juice and water, dry thoroughly, wrap, and refrigerate.

Make your own baby food. Check your library or bookstore for a how-to book. Freeze in ice cube trays to make convenient individual servings, then store them in sealable bags. (Exceptions to making your own are formula for newborns and rice cereal.)

Clean out and rearrange your pantry often. You won't believe the stuff you'll find hiding in the back. (Check the expiration dates.)

Use frozen orange juice concentrate instead of ready-to-drink. It's cheaper and it lasts longer.

Consider a vacuum sealing machine. Makes buying in bulk much more sensible. But don't buy one unless you're sure you'll use it.

Get a freezer. Too expensive? Consider sharing space with a neighbor or friend.

Keep your freezer full. A full freezer is an efficient freezer. If you don't have enough food to keep it jam-packed, fill plastic jugs with water (leave room for expansion) and freeze. You'll have fresh water in case of a power failure, and the frozen jugs will keep the freezer contents cold much longer.

Don't wash berries. They will freeze better if they aren't washed first. Any other washed fruit must be thoroughly dried before freezing.

Freeze strawberries whole. Remove leaves, but leave stems.

Use zip-type plastic bags for freezer containers. Squeeze out as much air as possible before zipping closed.

Keep a written index of freezer contents. Hang in a handy location. This way you can spend as much time as you need looking through inventory to make a decision without having the door open, letting in hot air.

Freeze items quickly. When putting things in the freezer, spread them out so all sides are in contact with the cold. When frozen, move everything together compactly.

Blanche vegetables before freezing. They contain enzymes that, if their action is not stopped, will cause the product to become coarse and flavorless. Enzymes defy freezing but cannot withstand heat. Before freezing, drop fresh vegetables into boiling water and transfer immediately into ice water. Work with small batches.

Properly wrap foods. Materials must be waterproof and moisture and vapor resistant to prevent food from drying out. Wrap very tightly, removing as much air as possible. Seal with tape.

Freeze these items:

Onions. Chop, then spread out in one layer on a cookie sheet. Place quickly in coldest place in freezer. When frozen, transfer to bag or container.

Mushrooms. Do not wash. Clean with bristle brush. Chop and freeze in same manner as onions.

Brown and powdered sugars. Prevents lumps.

Coffee. Either beans or ground. Maintains freshness.

Nuts. Retards spoilage. Nuts left in pantry will become rancid.

Popcorn kernels. The kernels will stay fresh much longer, and freezing will encourage every kernel to pop.

Marshmallows, potato chips, pretzels, and crackers. Works best if frozen in original unopened containers.

Clothing

Don't pay full price. With so many manufacturer outlets, discount mail-order catalogs, and fantastic sales, you should never pay the full retail price.

Buy fewer, but buy classic. Rethink your wardrobe to include fewer pieces. Make the few pieces classic items that look great year in and year out. Stay away from trends or fads.

Coordinate. Stick to a basic color scheme so you can mix and match to create more outfits with what you have.

Accessorize. Well-chosen accessories can turn the same basic dress or suit into four or five different looks.

Find a good tailor. Someone skilled at alterations can take in, let out, take up, let down, and redesign a classic and well-made garment.

Avoid "dry clean only." This kind of expensive maintenance will double or even triple the cost of a garment over the years.

Find a good, reasonable dry cleaner. Some cleaners charge a flat rate per item. Shop carefully.

Repair, resole, and reheel shoes. You can easily double or triple the life of a good pair of shoes with simple repairs. Do the same with luggage, handbags, and belts.

Recycle. Instead of having your children wear their siblings' hand-medowns, trade with neighbors or friends who have children of the same sizes. The kids get a new look, and the price is right.

Leave your good business shoes at the office. Change into an older pair when leaving to tromp up and down steps and out to the parking lot.

Shop at consignment stores. High-quality, previously owned clothes are sold at often 70 to 85 percent below the new price. Shop well and you will find unbelievable bargains.

Check out thrift shops. Never buy just because it's a good bargain. But if you have the time, you might be able to save a lot of money there.

Wash with cold water. Unless you are dealing with unusual stains, cold water and good detergent will clean just as well as warm or hot water. You'll save on hot water, the fabrics will last longer, and colors will stay bright much longer.

Change your clothes. As soon as you get home from work, change out of your expensive business suit and into casual clothing to minimize the chance of stains and snags.

Rent, don't buy, formal wear. Evening gowns, bridal dresses, and other formal wear are usually high priced—and worn once. So rent or, better yet, borrow. For men, tuxedo rental prices vary tremendously, so check around.

Stock up off-season. Seasonal items (swimwear, coats, boots, etc.) are often cleared out at phenomenal prices, so if you can handle the thought of buying snow wear in the spring, go for it!

Borrow maternity clothes. Start a co-op with your friends. Typically, maternity clothes don't get that much wear and are easy to maintain.

Become a stain-removal expert. Eliminating ugly stains may allow another year of wear.

Use shampoo on collar and cuff rings. Shampoo is meant to clean body oil, which causes rings around collars and cuffs. Baby shampoo is an excellent substitute for expensive cold-water soap.

Sew buttons on once and for all. Use dental floss for thread.

Avoid shopping at the last minute. Start planning ahead for your clothing needs. Last-minute stress is costly.

Ladies, buy men's white T-shirts to wear under jackets. They're cheap, easy to dye or trim, and are machine washable.

Think twice about leather, suede, and silk. They are lovely but expensive to maintain.

Hand wash delicates. Take them into the shower with you and use your shampoo on them.

Household

De-junk your home. If you are like most people, you have about twice as much stuff as you really like, use, or need. Have nothing in your home that you do not know to be useful or believe to be beautiful.

Learn to make repairs. Few household repairs are dangerous. Read manuals, take classes, be brave, and tackle the things that are not going to endanger your well-being.

Measure detergent for both washing machine and dishwasher. If you just dump it in, you are probably using way too much.

Recycle. Find new uses for things that are about to exceed their normal life span. For instance, worn-out bath towels make terrific car-washing rags. Worn-out socks and diapers make good dusters.

Use shaving cream as an upholstery cleaner. It's effective and cheap. Use it to spot-clean small areas.

Buy queen-size top sheets for king-size beds. King-size top sheets are usually way too big and require a lot of tucking in. Queen-size flats work great on most king-size beds and are a lot cheaper.

Buy sheets instead of yardage. Buying sheets on sale gives you extra-wide yardage at a fraction of the cost of yard goods. They're perfect for making curtains, tablecloths, napkins, pillows, nightclothes, and crafts.

Instead of buying finished area rugs, buy a remnant from a carpet store and have it bound. It's usually much cheaper.

Arrange for regular monthly bills to be paid directly out of your account by your bank. You'll save the costs of postage, late fees, checks, and envelopes.

Save receipts, warranties, and owner's manuals. Often these are all you will need to have an appliance repaired at no charge. Find a nifty binder that will keep everything neat and orderly.

Fire the maid. Get all the occupants of the house involved in cleaning. Learn speed-cleaning techniques.

Buy unfinished furniture. A little practice will go a long way, and usually, the store will give you a quick lesson. Buy the finishing products from a discount hardware store.

Beware of home shopping by television. The products are highly overpriced, overrated, and pitched to the compulsive shopper.

Learn to shop without buying. A little attitude change will allow you to thoroughly enjoy lovely things but leave them in the stores. Let someone else dust, polish, and care for them. You can visit "your" stuff whenever you like and change your mind without consequence!

Get friendly with salespeople. They usually know when things are going to go on sale. Ask and then be willing to wait.

Rent carpet cleaning equipment. Save big time by doing this chore yourself. You can usually rent better equipment than you could afford to own.

Clean the garage or basement. Hold a sale and get rid of what you don't use so you can organize what you do use.

Read magazines and books to learn cheap home decorating tricks. Picture framing, using sheets to make curtains and pillows, stenciling, and wallpapering are easy and fun. Look at the library for how-to books and publications.

Make your own cleaning products. Avoid the high-priced commercial products. Your library probably has several books that will tell you how to make environmentally safe and child-safe products.

Make dust cloths. Dip cheesecloth into a mixture of 2 cups water and 1/4 cup lemon oil. Let dry.

Clean silk flowers. Pop them into a paper bag with a small handful of uncooked rice. Shake to remove dust. Throw out the rice (who knows what was hiding in those flowers?).

Don't clean paint roller covers and brushes until your job is completely finished. Just wrap them tightly in plastic wrap overnight (or a couple of days) and keep them in the freezer. They'll stay soft and usable until you're ready to finish.

Store partially full cans of paint upside down. The paint will form an airtight seal, extending the useful life.

To remove ugly oil stains on your driveway, sprinkle with kitty litter and scrub with a brick. Repeat for stubborn stains.

Make your own household deodorizer. Put a cinnamon stick or a few whole cloves in vacuum cleaner bag to make your house smell clean and fresh. (Doesn't work unless you actually run the vacuum!)

Remove ink marks from plastic. Spray with hair spray and wipe clean.

Sharpen scissors. Cut through a piece of 220 grit sandpaper.

Utilities

Buy energy efficient. When selecting a new appliance, look for the yellow tag with the "EER" on it. The higher the number, the less wasteful of energy and more efficient it is.

Preheat oven only if the recipe tells you to. Casseroles and roasts don't suffer from starting out cold.

Let your fingers do the walking, even if it requires a toll call. It's cheaper than driving your car.

Check to see if you have deposits on account. Usually if you have been a good customer (gas, water, electricity, phone) for at least a year, you can arrange to have your deposits refunded or credited toward your account. You may be able to get interest, too, if you ask.

If someone in your family has a vision impairment, try to get free directory assistance.

Take short showers instead of water-guzzling baths.

Install a flow-controlling showerhead. Your kids will never notice, but your water bill will.

If your phone service is interrupted for more than 24 hours, ask for a credit. You'll probably get it, especially if you nicely point out that you pay dearly for the privilege of having a telephonic link to the outside world.

Always check for a toll-free number before dialing long distance. It's free to call 800 Directory Assistance (1-800-555-1212).

Close off seldom-used rooms. This way you don't have to heat them in cold weather or cool them during the hot months.

Conserve electricity by using a carpet sweeper (one of those push-type gizmos with brush rollers) instead of vacuuming every day. Vacuuming once a week will probably be more than sufficient for deep cleaning.

Substitute a fluffy comforter for your electricity-sucking electric blanket.

Put an egg timer by the phone. The timer will remind you to hang up before you talk yourself into debt oblivion.

Call corporate collect. Try it. Most large companies will accept your collect call as a matter of course. Just identify yourself as a good customer or potential client. If denied, just call back direct. Hey, it's worth a try, and it usually works.

Always ask for credit immediately upon dialing a wrong number. Don't be embarrassed. It's routine.

Have a phone checkup annually. Request an equipment inventory report. The phone company will send you a form listing the services for which you are charged. If you find you've been overpaying, demand a retroactive refund.

Consider having the telephone company block 900 numbers. They are never free and can cost as much as $20 a minute.

Turn off the oven or stove right before an item is completely finished. Whatever heat is left is usually enough to finish the job.

Use glass or ceramic for baking. If you use these kinds of dishes in the oven, you can lower heat by up to 25 degrees from what's called for by recipes.

Check that the stove burner equals pan size. The pan should completely cover the burner to avoid energy waste.

Use three-way bulbs. They are more efficient provided you use the lower wattage whenever possible. Dimmer switches are good energy conservers as well.

Don't open fridge or freezer until you are sure what you are going after.

Replace cracked or loose gasket around refrigerator door.

Run only full dishwasher. Otherwise you're wasting precious hot water and electricity.

Don't leave the coffeepot warming for hours on end. Instead, transfer finished coffee to a thermos and turn that energy-sucker off.

Keep water heater at about 120 degrees (midrange). Water will wash just as efficiently and will be less apt to scald.

Run the dishwasher in the evening and turn off before dry cycle. Open door and allow dishes to air dry overnight.

Wrap blanket-type insulation around water heater. Savings over the first year will probably more than pay for the blanket.

Draw drapes or close awnings to cut down on heating and air-conditioning. Drapes act as great insulators.

Put up storm windows and check weather stripping around doors and windows. Anything you can do to make your home airtight will reduce your heating/cooling bills.

Insulate your basement to prevent loss of heat and cool. The cost should be recouped within three years.

Get a utility checkup. Many utility companies will send representatives to your home and give you free advice on how you can conserve energy better.

Use fabric wall hangings. A quilt or decorative rug will insulate interior walls and keep your room cozier with the thermostat turned down.

If you leave a room for more than 15 minutes, turn off the lights.

Cook topside whenever possible. Stove or range top uses less energy than your oven.

Choose smaller appliances. Electric skillets or woks, slow cookers, and pressure cookers use less energy than a range or oven.

Set refrigerator thermostat at 38 to 40 degrees Fahrenheit. This is probably about 10 degrees higher than recommended by manufacturer but can cut running costs by almost 25 percent. To get similar savings from the freezer, set it between 0 and 5 degrees Fahrenheit.

Vacuum the coils at the bottom or back of your refrigerator frequently to prevent dust from building up around them. Dust makes the refrigerator run more often and so does keeping it too close to the wall. The refrigerator and freezer need room to breathe or else they get too hot and run too much.

Turn off curling iron, clothes iron, coffeepot, etc., when not in use.

When baking, keep track of cooking time with a timer. Don't keep peeking into the oven. Each peek can cost as much as 25 degrees Fahrenheit; it can also affect browning and baking.

Install timers and/or motion detectors rather than leaving lights on all night. This will ensure you're using lights only when necessary.

Fill a small, plastic bottle with water. Place it in your toilet tank away from the flushing mechanism. This will require less water volume in the tank, and your toilet will still flush just fine.

Buy your own phone. Renting from the phone company is very expensive.

Consider energy-efficient lightbulbs. They cost more up front, but you will save a lot over the long term.

Make sure your lightbulbs are the correct wattage for the appliance. Putting a 150-watt bulb in a 75-watt socket wastes energy, and it could cause a fire.

Reacquaint yourself with a clothesline. Hanging out a few loads of laundry each week instead of using a gas or electric clothes dryer can save hundreds of dollars each year.

Turn water heater way down when away on vacation.

Install water-saving toilets when you need to replace your old ones. Check with your utility company. Many offer rebates in excess of the cost of a new commode just for your trouble.

Check for leaks. Drop a little food coloring into the toilet tank. If any color shows up in the bowl, you have a leak. Fix it.

Water your lawn at night. Sunshine encourages evaporation. By watering at night, more water will stay on the lawn and penetrate into the roots, allowing your watering time to be shorter than during daylight hours.

Close fireplace damper unless you have a fire going.

Check out your phone bill. Phone companies are not perfect, and chances are you've been paying for someone else's phone calls.

Call during cheapest hours. Usually nights and weekends.

Avoid directory assistance. It's amazing that phone companies actually charge for that, but they do. Get a phone book and use it.

Use postcards to communicate on non-urgent matters. They're much cheaper than a long-distance phone call.

Put your phone service on "vacation" while you are out of town. The savings are modest, but every little bit helps.

Reconsider all the phone add-ons. Maybe you aren't even using some of the features you're paying for (call waiting, call forwarding, speed dialing, etc.).

Buy heating oil off-season. Start checking prices in the spring. Typically, you should be able to take advantage of lowest prices from July to September. The same applies to firewood.

Freeze before you freeze. This works only if you live in a cold climate. Putting room temperature items in your refrigerator or freezer actually heats up the environment in there for a while. During the winter months, put these items outdoors to cool before going into fridge or freezer.

Insurance

Take higher deductibles. In essence, you partially self-insure by being willing to take the chance that you won't get sick, you won't crash the car, or you won't be burglarized. The higher the deductible, the lower the premium. The insurance company actually compensates the customer who is willing to share a greater portion of the risk.

Commute by car pool. Most insurance companies offer discounts to low-mileage drivers.

Stay out of the death lane. The far left lane is where speeders hang out and most accidents occur.

Drive for five drivers: yourself, drivers in front, at both sides, and behind you. Be prepared for them to do the unexpected.

Have adequate protection. With the higher deductibles, you can afford better coverage, which is a wise move.

Find a company that gives discounts for having all of your types of insurance with the same company. Insurance companies can offer volume discounts.

Call your agent every year. Make sure your agent has all of the correct information—including your teenage son's good driving record and three years' experience. All of these things might matter.

Install a timer on a radio as well as on outdoor and indoor lights. Timers are cheap protection. Burglars tend to avoid a home if they think there's a chance someone's around.

Don't be predictable. A car that's always parked in the same place for the same amount of time each day or night lets thieves know where to look for it and how much time they'd need to make off with it.

Ask about discounts for security systems, smoke alarms, good driving records, etc. Always ask! The agent or company may not volunteer the information.

Add a replacement-cost rider to renter or home owner insurance. It may cost a little more, but in case of a claim, you will be glad you did. Without it, the company will depreciate the value of every item, and you will be a big loser.

Consider umbrella liability. It is very cheap and could be a lifesaver, especially if you have kids and your exposure is great. Check with your agent.

Don't make small claims. Too many can lead to policy cancellations or premium hikes. Insurance companies think that a frequent filer is heading for a serious accident.

File for diminution of value against the other guy's insurance company if the damage to your car was the other guy's fault. Even though it is repaired adequately, the car has a diminished resale value for which you should be compensated. On average, you can file for 10 percent of the total repair cost. Be persistent.

Don't buy travel insurance. It's one of the biggest rip-offs.

If possible, pay premiums annually. Avoid the added costs for monthly or quarterly billing.

Don't put insurance policies in a safe deposit vault. These boxes are often sealed by court order when the box holder dies. That could cause a substantial delay.

If you're single, buy life insurance only if someone is financially dependent on you.

Scrutinize your deck sheet with every renewal. This is the coverage sheet that shows your limits. Don't overinsure. Computers have a way of sneaking stuff in.

Make sure you are with a highly rated company. These days the smaller, lower-rated companies are dropping out regularly. Better safe than sorry.

Buy term life insurance. Experts that I trust advise that whole life and universal life are not wise investments. Check with your own professional—but do check.

Don't buy life insurance for kids. It makes absolutely no sense. Insure only wage earners (including stay-home moms!) whose untimely departure would create a financial hardship.

Don't buy too much life insurance. Make sure it is adequate to maintain current lifestyles and needs. Don't let your agent decide how much you need. He wants to make a big sale! You decide. Insurance companies will say that a family needs at least enough life insurance to cover four or five times its yearly income.

Cut back on life insurance as your dependents become independent. Providing for a spouse alone costs less than a spouse and eight kids!

Never buy insurance from television or direct mail ads. This is a sleazy marketing ploy. The premiums are at least 400 percent too high for the coverage, and the exclusions are mammoth.

Drop your comprehensive and collision insurance when the value of your car drops below $2,500. Save the difference in premiums to buy another car.

Videotape your home inside and out for insurance records. In case of a fire, you need to have evidence of the expensive wall coverings and decorator window coverings. While you are taping, narrate aloud and describe in detail. Keep the tape in a safe deposit box. Make sure video date is well documented. Revideo every few years or when considerable changes are made. Tapes don't last forever either.

If you rent, buy a tenant's policy. This is a must. Landlords are not responsible for your belongings in case of disaster.

Never buy credit disability insurance, automobile service contracts, extended warranties on appliances and electronics, or Chargegard (for credit cards).

Never buy mortgage life insurance. This is the kind of policy tied to your mortgage or other credit purchase that will pay off the balance in case of your death. If you think you need the additional insurance, arrange it yourself, and leave your heirs the choice of paying off the mortgage or not.

Transportation

Think long and hard before buying new. Since financing charges are so great, paying cash is the method of choice, and new cars are expensive.

Research. Check *Consumer Reports* and other publications to learn all you can before making a decision.

Buy at a slow sales time. February is the best month to buy because consumers are worn out and dealers try to get their attention with sales. The second best time is two weeks before Christmas. Terrible weather provides a good time to make a deal.

Choose a car not coveted by criminals. A phone call to your local police department will reveal which are the most-stolen cars in your area.

Don't carry more than you need. A light load gets much better gas mileage. Clean out heavy items from the trunk, and leave only the spare tire and safety equipment. Don't make your car a mobile warehouse for stuff you can leave in the garage.

Avoid roof and trunk racks. These things ruin aerodynamics and cut gas mileage.

Never drive when angry or upset. Angry drivers waste fuel, are dangerous to themselves and others on the road, and are hard on the engine.

Listen to traffic reports to avoid tie-ups and congestion. You may be able to change routes and avoid costly congestion.

Reduce warm-up time. A 30-second warm-up is sufficient for modern cars. Any longer and you are just wasting precious fuel.

Be gentle and keep it steady. A light foot on the accelerator will certainly save fuel.

Slow down. Not only will you get optimum performance, but you may avoid a costly ticket and unfortunate insurance increases.

Be diligent about regular scheduled maintenance. It pays off every day. It makes parts last longer, prevents most emergency breakdowns, and promotes good gas mileage.

Be observant. Look, listen, and sniff occasionally for anything unusual about your car. You know your car best, and early diagnosis will pay off later. Take note of odd noises, hard starting, or significant loss of power.

Have your brakes replaced before the rotors have to be turned. You'll save hundreds of dollars. Your mechanic should check for free and tell you how much of the pad is remaining. Don't push it past 5 percent.

Check your own fluid levels. Just a little time and patience will go a long way to keep engine, brakes, and transmission in tip-top shape. Make sure you have a reliable teacher.

Learn how to do some of your regular maintenance. Books, video-tapes, colleges, and adult schools all can teach you about routine maintenance. It's not so hard to fix a car—the hard part is figuring out what's wrong!

Find a professional you can trust to handle the major stuff. Don't be afraid to get a second opinion.

Check battery terminals. Corroded battery terminals can leave you stranded. Quick fix: Pour a cola drink or other carbonated beverage over the terminals. It will eat through the corrosion. This is a temporary measure to get you where you need to go without a tow.

Keep tires inflated properly. Underinflated tires drag down gas mileage; overinflated ones cause premature wear. Don't forget to check the spare, too.

Buy the smallest car you can live with. Weight is the biggest enemy of fuel economy.

Keep your cars longer. Proper maintenance will allow you to keep a car for 10 years or longer. My professional insists that if maintained right, a car should serve faithfully for more than 300,000 miles.

Use public transportation whenever possible. It's still cheaper than driving your own, especially if you are alone.

Rent. If you live in a big city with good public transportation, sell your car and rent one on the rare occasions when you really need one. You'll save on insurance, wear and tear, and parking.

Sell an extra car. Do you really need two, three, or four cars?

Pay cash for used. It makes much better sense than financing a new auto. Auto loans carry huge interest rates.

Skip the vanity license plates. Find a cheaper way to promote yourself.

Check on insurance rates before you make a decision. Call your agent with a couple of choices and get quotes.

Avoid fancy options. They just mean that there are many more expensive things to go wrong.

Try to get yellow rear turn signals. Research suggests that cars with yellow turn signals are less likely to be hit from behind while turning than cars with red signals.

Never agree to buy dealer's options. Extended warranties, fancy paint job protectors, racing stripes, sunroofs—these are huge profit items for the dealer.

Don't lease. Leasing only encourages trading in more often. Even the best lease is going to cost you more in the long run.

Don't trade in your old car. Sell it yourself. The dealer will probably never give you what you can get for it from an individual buyer.

Drive with the windows closed. Open windows mess up aerodynamics and cost you more in gas mileage than running the air conditioner.

Pump your own gas. Full serve is outrageously more expensive. Keep a box of disposable plastic gloves handy so you don't smell like a service station attendant all day.

Inspect your fan belts. Carry a spare or two in your trunk.

Wash and wax your car yourself or teach your kids how. Professional car washes are very expensive.

Buy oil and other fluids in bulk at the discount store. Buying oil a quart at a time at the service station is not smart.

Pay registration renewals on time. Most states hand out heavy penalties if you are even one day late.

If you rent a car, reject offers of additional optional coverage. Be prepared for some heavy-handed tactics to get you to accept it. Salespersons get hefty bonuses if you can be persuaded.

Don't throw away empty tissue boxes. They make wonderful caddies for the car. They are the perfect size to hold sunglasses, lotion, spare change, and cassette tapes and can be used for a trash receptacle in the car. They are also good storage boxes for crayons, doll clothes, and puzzle pieces.

Home Owners and Renters

If you have an extra room, consider taking in a boarder to help defray your costs. Post a notice (for free) at a local community college or corporation. Check with personnel offices at larger corporations in your area. Often they assist employees in locating affordable housing.

Get more than one bid for major repairs or improvements.

Don't fall for scams. They usually come in the form of door-to-door salespersons.

Don't overbuild the neighborhood. Usually, the most expensive house in the neighborhood appreciates the least.

Carefully choose location. Location is the most important criterion in selecting a home.

Drive a hard bargain when you purchase a home. Get help from friends or relatives who are less emotionally involved.

Negotiate the closing costs. Always ask for more than you are willing to accept.

Make sure you earn interest on your deposit during the escrow period.

Never allow the seller to select inspectors. You want an impartial assessment of possible termite damage, roof condition, plumbing and electrical situations, and structural soundness.

Make sure the escrow holder is truly impartial. Often the seller's broker will steer the escrow to a company in which he or she has some financial interest. It is better to have an escrow with no ties.

Have your head examined before you attempt to build your own home. Unless you are a developer or professional contractor, you are in for a big surprise, not the least of which is that it could cost twice what you estimate.

Change smoke detector batteries on your birthday. Also, vacuum the detector to get dust and dirt out of sensors. Smoke detectors don't last forever, so make sure you test yours often and replace it readily.

Move into a smaller house. The lower costs could drastically improve your financial situation.

Use students and other nonprofessionals for odd jobs such as moving furniture, gardening, painting, carpentry, and any other

jobs that you cannot do. Call your local college or university and ask for the job placement office.

Sell by owner. Prepare for lots of aggravation and allow time to research and learn how. You can save significant dollars.

Shop your mortgage. Programs vary a great deal. Get many opinions.

Refinance your existing mortgage. If you plan to stay in the house for the next two to three years and you can beat your present interest rate by 1.5 percent, it may be a good idea. Consider the points on the new loan. Try to negotiate the closing costs and points if possible.

Pay more than the monthly payment. This is probably one of the best things you can do with extra cash. You will pay down the principal more quickly, which will result in a tremendous saving of interest.

Instead of paying your mortgage monthly, pay half of your mortgage payment every two weeks. You will end up making 26 half-payments, which equal 13 monthly payments. Your spending plan will absorb this additional payment with little, if any, pain, and your principal will love you.

Do your own painting and decorating. Check out home improvement centers to learn the latest techniques.

If you are going to sell your home at a loss, try and hold off a while and rent it out so that you can take advantage of the tax loss when you eventually sell. Check with your accountant. If you can show it as an investment rather than personal residence, you might be able to recoup some of the loss.

Challenge your property tax bill. If your value has declined, you might be entitled to a reassessment of your taxes.

Clean out gutters. Be careful. It's a little tricky, especially with a two-story home. You may, though, prevent some drainage problems in the future.

Remember your one-time $125,000 exclusion on capital gains if you are 55 or older.

Check with your city. Sometimes low-interest or grant money is available for modernizing or fixing up the outside. Be the first in line.

If you have a home business, a portion of your mortgage and related expenses may be taken as a tax deduction. It's tricky, so get professional advice.

Install automatic timers on your sprinkler systems. Water less often for a longer period of time to allow deep penetration.

If you rent, find an area with rent control. If the law is in place, you might as well take advantage of it.

Get a roommate so you can afford a nicer, bigger place. Make sure to put in writing the details of your agreement about who pays for what.

Negotiate the rent. In a market where many vacancies exist, the tenant is king.

Be clear about your rental agreement before you sign anything. Deposits should be clearly spelled out. Ask for interest to be paid on deposits.

Before you vacate, take extra pains to clean. No one wants a hassle over return of deposits. The landlord will give you a good recommendation in the future, and that is valuable.

Health and Personal Care

Get your hair cut, colored, or curled at a beauty school. Students are usually carefully supervised, conscientious, and anxious to please. Be nice but firm about your expectations and desires. Prices are unbelievably low.

Take advantage of store testers and free samples. These are often available at cosmetic counters. Buying before trying is a waste.

Use plain talcum instead of expensive perfumed bath powder.

Stand nearly empty bottles of hand lotion, moisturizer, and other creamy stuff upside down. The cap will accumulate enough to last another week or so.

Learn to cut your kids' hair. Learn well from someone who is good at it. You'll save at least $75 a year per kid.

Don't get sick. Practice preventive health maintenance now. Even with the best insurance, you are going to end up paying for deductibles, copayments, and prescriptions.

Never be without health insurance. High deductibles are fine because you intend to stay healthy. But one catastrophic illness or accident could wipe out everything you have saved and planned for.

Brush and floss daily. Preventive dental care is easy to practice. You can avoid costly gum disease, bridges, and dentures by simply brushing, flossing, and rinsing often.

Keep kids' immunizations up to date. Sick kids mean parents must miss work or pay for expensive alternative day-care. The costs really add up. Most can be prevented.

Look for free or cheap immunization programs through your local health department.

Make your own flexible ice packs. Pour 3/4 cup water and 1/4 cup rubbing alcohol into a zip-type plastic bag and close. Put zipped bag into another bag, seal, and freeze. You will have a slushy bag of ice whenever needed for sprains, headaches, or whatever.

Shop health insurance coverage. Often the first-year premium is much less, so changing is not a bad idea. If your employer offers a menu of coverages, check them all carefully. A health maintenance organization (HMO) might be best for your particular situation.

Always get a second opinion for any major medical procedure. Doctors are human and have been known to make mistakes.

Carefully examine hospital bills. If you go in for a knee reconstruction and are billed for infant nursery time, put up a fuss. Hospitals are notorious for making these kinds of mistakes.

Find a walk-in clinic for emergencies. These 24-hour clinics are popping up all over and are much cheaper than hospital emergency rooms.

Take your own stuff to the hospital. If your doctor approves, you can arrange to take your own food, prescriptions (have doctor write these out ahead of time so you can pick them up at your discount pharmacy), TV, cellular phone (rent one), and toiletry items. Insist on an a la carte plan so you pay the absolute bare minimum. But be prepared: It's still going to cost a lot to be hospitalized.

If you have to be admitted to a hospital, insist that you go in the day of the surgery. An early admittance will run up your bill and is usually for the convenience of the staff, not the patient.

Inquire about specific hospital fees before you are admitted. Fees do vary considerably from one hospital to the next. Why pay for the availability of kidney machines and heart transplant teams if you are having knee reconstruction?

Ask questions. Seventy-five percent of all antibiotics taken each year are unnecessary. Doctors know that patients who take the time and trouble to make an office visit expect to be "rewarded" with a prescription! Doctors like to keep their patients happy, too. Ask the prescribing doctor exactly what the prescription can and cannot do for you and if it is necessary for full recovery.

Always consider generic. Ask your doctor to prescribe the cheapest form of medicine.

Shop prescriptions. I have found that pharmacies will quote prices over the phone. Call around. You won't believe how the prices vary.

Ask your doctor for free samples. Pharmaceutical companies flood doctors with samples of all kinds of expensive prescriptions. If your doctor doesn't offer, ask.

Buy routine prescriptions through the mail. Many mail-order pharmacies fill prescriptions on a 48-hour basis.

Keep track of parking fees and mileage associated with medical care for tax purposes.

Make a cheap and effective facial mask with milk of magnesia.

Mix baking soda with a little water to get a great facial scrub.

Spritz feet and inside of shoes with rubbing alcohol in a spray bottle. It's very refreshing and eliminates foot odor.

Soak your fingertips in a 50/50 mixture of warm water and white vinegar before applying nail polish. It will last much longer.

Try applying a wet, black tea bag to a nasty canker sore. The tannin acts as an astringent and will relieve the pain and promote healing.

Prevent canker sores by adding four tablespoons of plain yogurt to your diet each day.

Don't smoke. Even a smoking habit that isn't excessive will cost around $1,000 a year and who-knows-how-much more in additional health care.

Take vitamins. Especially take vitamin C, which has been proven to help stave off colds and flu, lower cholesterol, decrease arthritis pain, reduce outbreaks of canker sores, and lessen premenstrual syndrome, just to name a few benefits. Staying healthy may eliminate expensive doctor visits.

Buy a book on home remedies. Make sure it is written by competent doctors and then memorize it! *The Doctor's Book of Home Remedies* (Rodale Press) is a great one, I've found.

Make your own hot water bottle. Fill a two-liter plastic soda pop bottle about four inches from the top with hot tap water. Replace screw-top tightly. Wrap in terry cloth towel and snuggle up.

Kids and Families

Don't get divorced. A divorce most certainly will have a damaging effect on your finances, to say nothing of your emotions. Just imagine the problem of running two households on what it takes to support one now.

Don't lend money to a friend. It's just too risky to your financial health and your friendship.

Don't lend money to family members. Consider it a gift, and if you just happen to get paid back, it's a bonus.

Open school savings accounts for your kids. Teach them how to fill out deposit slips and make their own deposits. These accounts usually have no minimum balances or service fees.

Share baby-sitting. Work out a plan with your friends to trade favors. Consider starting a baby-sitting co-op. Do research on others that have been successful.

Teach kids to make lunches. Brown bagging is a good idea—even for Mom and Dad.

Acquaint your family with the local public library. Current newspapers, magazines, children's books, adult books, videos, CDs, wonderful story-telling librarians—what a fabulous place the library is. And it's *free*. If you like to shop for fun, satisfy the impulse by visiting a library. You get to take home something new, and it doesn't cost anything!

Find free entertainment. Family outings do not have to be expensive. Biking, hiking, visiting a park or playground, going on picnics, and attending free concerts are just a few suggestions.

Move to an area with excellent public schools. Save the cost of private school tuition.

Trade toys. Find a family with kids about the same age as yours. Do a toy swap. "New" toys for free! (Save them up for Christmas and birthdays.) This works best with younger kids.

Take your own snacks to movies and ball games.

Go to a movie matinee. It's always cheaper!

Rent a movie instead of springing for tickets for the entire family.

Don't join record, CD, or book clubs. You can do much better at your local discount stores, and you won't have to worry about sending back selections you didn't want.

When buying kids' clothes and shoes, set a budget figure, and if the child wants to upgrade to a trendier brand or style, require her or him to pay the difference.

Perfect reverse psychology. It comes in handy as an effective way of steering adolescents away from expensive tastes.

Dream big. It's free!

Miscellaneous

Plant deciduous (lose their leaves in winter) trees on the south side of your house. They will provide summer shade without blocking winter sun.

Plant evergreens on the north to shield your home from cold winter winds.

Put cut flowers in the refrigerator when you're at work, asleep, or otherwise unable to enjoy them.

Ask your dry cleaner or neighborhood repair shops to let you know when they have unclaimed goods for sale. There are terrific bargains.

Request a discount whenever you pay cash in a store that honors standard bank credit cards. Since they have to pay from 3 to 7 percent of the bill to the card company on a credit purchase, they should be willing to give you at least part of the difference in the form of a discount. It won't always work, but it's worth a try.

When staying in a hotel, don't make phone calls from your room. Use the pay phone in the lobby and save at least 50 percent, even on your local calls.

Don't carry extra cash. Take along only as much money as you expect to need each day. Impulsive purchases are difficult to make with no dollars to spare.

Think positively. Think about how much you are gaining from your cheapskate lifestyle, not what you are giving up.

Shop for a free checking account. Most banks have them if you ask. There may be certain stipulations, but usually, they are quite easy to adhere to. Senior citizens are usually entitled to free accounts without limits.

When entertaining guests for a meal, spend time, not money. The biggest compliment you can pay your dinner guests is to serve dishes that require more preparation than money. Anyone can grill an expensive steak or roast a rack of lamb, but few people make beef bourguignon, lasagna, soufflés, homemade breads, cheesecakes, or other time-consuming dishes, despite how delicious and economical they can be. The hostess who goes to the trouble to prepare such delicacies gives her guests, her family, and her spending plan a treat.

Vacation during off-season. You can save big time on everything from travel to hotels and food.

Take up camping. Borrow or rent the gear.

Attend free concerts. Most cities have community-sponsored entertainment during summer months. Many churches and colleges have free performances during holidays.

Work hard. Be a good employee and give a full day's work for a full day's pay. Keep your job.

Be content with what you have. As much as possible, do not spend your life scheming and planning to get more things.

Never buy checks through your bank. You can save more than 50 percent by ordering direct.

Find a bank that doesn't charge a fee for ATM activity. If this is impossible, curb the urge to make many small transactions.

Take it back. If you bought something that you can't use, you don't like, or is damaged, for heaven's sake, take it back. Retailers these days are quite anxious to make the customer happy by making adjustments, giving credit or cash refunds. Decide what you want and then stand up for yourself.

Have your pet neutered. Nursing, feeding, and finding homes for litters are costly, both emotionally and financially.

Collect loose change. Make it a habit to dump your pockets and purses every night into one collection receptacle. You won't miss the change, and you'll be amazed how much you can save.

Convince yourself that debt is a four-letter word. As soon as you teach that to yourself, teach it to your children. Banish it from your life. (Debt here is understood to be unsecured consumer credit.)

Replace an item only if you cannot refurbish, repair, redo, or get along without.

Barter. Whenever possible, trade goods or services instead of money: haircuts for typing, baby-sitting for landscape maintenance, or housecleaning for electrical work.

Do not carry credit cards. If you have to own them, keep them in a safe, out-of-the-way place.

Think about it for 30 days before you sign. Any purchase that requires your signature probably requires payments. You just might have a change of heart. If not, then you probably will avoid buyer's remorse and feel confident in your decision.

Chapter 11

Difficult Situations

What to Do with Less-Than-Tidy
Circumstances

E ven if you follow the Money Makeover plan that I've outlined, you still might encounter problems and situations that trip you up. Let's take a look at some of the difficult situations you might find yourself in.

No-Fault Financial Problems

Not everyone's financial situation is a result of poor money management. Perhaps your troubles stem from huge medical bills not covered by insurance. Maybe you are a single parent trying to survive on a

below-poverty-level income. My recommendation is that you follow the
principles of the Money Makeover as much as possible, and then not be
ashamed to seek assistance from outside sources. In this country,
charitable organizations and governmental agencies might be able to help
you. Of course, your best tactic is still to find new ways to cut expenses.

Self-Employment

If you look to commission sales or other forms of self-employment as
your sole source of income, the words *roller coaster* probably bring more
to mind than a large, steel edifice at Six Flags Over Somewhere. And I
would not be surprised if because of your status, you have dismissed most
of what you have read thus far as inapplicable to your situation. Having
been self-employed most of my working years, I know exactly the justifi-
cations for being unable to plan ahead or stick with a plan.

The majority of those who fall into the irregular income category live in
constant uncertainty. Some months can produce absolutely no income,
then a deal closes or a big account comes through, resulting in a good-
sized check, which usually is applied in its entirety to catching up. During
those particularly wonderful months, the entitlement mentality kicks in,
demanding that something extravagant be purchased. Somehow when the
big deal closes, we forget about the lean months and the fact that there
may be many more ahead.

"Feast or famine" sums it up. For many, at least in the beginning, self-
employment is survival on a daily basis. "Self-employeds" usually conclude
it is impossible to come up with any kind of reasonable spending plan or
to live within one's means when the means are so unpredictable. But this
is wrong!

Commissioned salespersons, freelancers, and small business owners
make a huge mistake when they fail to become their own strict and
unbending employer. Those of us in this position must wear two different
hats—that of employer and that of employee.

As the employee, you need to determine honestly what is the lowest
reasonable amount you can accept from yourself, the employer, as
monthly compensation. Now that's a new twist. Usually, self-employed

people ask, "What is the largest amount I can possibly pull out of this business every month?" Let's say, for example, that your rock-bottom, absolutely minimum figure is $3,000 a month, based upon your Monthly Spending Plan. You may intend to bring $10 million into the business this year, but determining your reasonable monthly requirements has nothing to do with that. As your employer, you must determine if the "business" (this applies to commissioned salespeople, too, who should see themselves as self-employed) is able to commit to this $3,000 monthly salary for its favorite "employee." Let's assume that it can.

Next, you must open another checking account. If you are a typical small-business owner, you take varying sums of money (depending upon current need or availability) directly from the business account and deposit them into your personal checking account. The amount probably fluctuates greatly from month to month. As a freelance artist or commissioned salesperson, you have been used to depositing your commission checks or payments directly into your personal account. This is a problem!

By opening another checking account, you will be able to take control. Example: You receive a $10,000 commission check in January, nothing in February, and nothing in March; in April you receive four checks for $550, $1,200, $3,000, and $850. Not so bad. That's $15,600 for four months, which should more than cover your expenses of $3,000 a month. The problem is, in January you might have had to play catch-up on all of the holiday bills that you couldn't pay because December was a "dry" month. And then there were all of those great after-Christmas sales, and you felt as if you had extra money so you splurged a bit here and there. Along come February and March and no income. The personal checking account is depleted, the credit cards are called into action, and it's desperation time until April. The $5,600 received in April barely gets you caught up, and so goes the ride on the roller coaster.

With the new checking account method, here is what would happen: The January $10,000 check would not be deposited into the regular checking account. Instead it would go into the holding account (or whatever you want to call it). You would become a strict and stern employer and guard this account as any good employer or business owner would. On "payday"—that is, a predetermined day that you pay yourself each month—you write yourself, the employee, a paycheck for $3,000, regardless of the balance in that account. After all, as your own employee you can't expect a raise every month. It's $3,000 (or whatever the amount you have previously negotiated with yourself) on payday, and that's it. On February 1, you write yourself a $3,000 paycheck. On March 1, you write yourself a $3,000 paycheck. On April 1, you deposit the $5,600 and write yourself a $3,000 paycheck, and so on each month.

If your self-employment work is sufficient to support you and your family, you should not have to worry. The income flowing into the holding account should exceed the paychecks. As the holding account becomes healthy, there will be additional funds to carry you through lean times. When things are going well and there are sufficient reserves, you might even consider sitting down with yourself to negotiate a raise, but don't be too hasty. Weigh the pros and cons. Consider the position of the prudent employer and the needy employee.

The self-employed person's major problem is the temptation to live it up when a big check comes in. After all, surely a bigger and better deal is just around the corner that will take care of the future. You seem to be living within your means, but don't be deceived. Your success as a self-employed person lies in your ability to discipline yourself and be a fair but strict employer and at the same time a grateful, restrained employee.

Negotiating with Creditors

What happens when one's financial situation becomes so dire that even after doing everything we've discussed (keeping impeccable spending records, setting up a Freedom Account, cutting expenses to bare minimum, and incurring no new debt) ends still don't meet? What happens when there's nothing left to cut, no hope of increasing income, and no more assets to liquidate?

The following suggestions are for only the most desperate situations. Unless you have honestly tried every tactic to bring your spending in line with your income and kept impeccable spending records for at least four months, you probably shouldn't even be reading this.

This is for those critical situations in which declaring bankruptcy seems to be the best alternative, but you are willing to try one last possibility.

Look at your list of debts. There's no doubt they are killing you. Minimum monthly payments may exceed your total income. By now these creditors are sick of hearing your stories and promises, and you're just as sick of hearing their threats. Perhaps you've been avoiding their calls, allowing their collection tactics to ruin your day and throw you into depression.

Look back at your Monthly Spending Plan. Ignoring your Freedom Account and Rapid Debt-Repayment Plan, what is the total of your *essential* monthly expenses? (I assume that you have cut this to the bare bone, and that this number represents only your basic needs.) When you deduct these expenses from your average monthly income, how much is left? If it isn't enough to pay your minimum monthly debt payments, how close is it? To find out, divide the amount of money left over after paying for essential monthly expenses by the total of your minimum monthly debt payments. That will give you a percentage. Let's say for illustration purposes it is 60 percent. You can't pay 100 percent of your monthly payments on your debts, but you can pay 60 percent.

I am not about to propose that any of your creditors waive payments. I'm suggesting that given the right set of circumstances, your creditors might be willing to work with you to renegotiate the terms of your payback. But you must approach them in a mature, sincere, and responsible manner, and you may have to ask forgiveness for your past behavior.

First, you need to look deeply into your heart. Are you willing to keep whatever promise you make to your creditors? If you cannot embrace integrity as part of your new makeover, you will not succeed.

None of this is going to be easy. I hate confrontations, and you probably do, too. My knees get weak and my voice trembles when I have to make difficult phone calls. I find writing letters to be easier, but not always as effective.

Look at your Rapid Debt-Repayment Plan. First, take each of your minimum monthly debt payments and multiply by the percentage you can pay. Next, contact each of your creditors and tell them, "I have a real financial problem. I don't want to declare bankruptcy. I've entered into a financial recovery program. I have come up with a plan that I am dedicated to working with and a repayment plan to which I am committed. I do not want you to suffer, and I am determined to pay back every single cent I owe you. I intend to pay you 60 percent [or the percentage you have determined] of my current monthly payment. I promise to pay you the same amount every month even if my required minimum payment drops. I need your help."

I have provided a sample letter (below) that would be appropriate to send to each of your creditors. Feel free to use it verbatim on one condition: You must be willing to carry through and make every promised payment. This is a serious letter, and you should not use it without a great deal of thought.

The letter ends with an "assumptive close." You are asking for a favor and are assuming it will be granted, and as such, you are acting as if it has been accepted. You must enclose a check or money order to demonstrate your good faith and commitment.

Creditor Name
Creditor Address
Date

RE: Account

Dear Sirs,

I (or we, as appropriate) am writing to you about my account as referenced above. I deeply regret that I have fallen behind and have failed to abide by the terms of our agreement. I want you to know that I am committed to full repayment in the amount of $_____.

I have recently undertaken a financial recovery program and have assessed my financial situation, and as a result, I have created a full repayment plan. I am doing everything I possibly can to avoid filing for bankruptcy.

Your account, unfortunately, is only one of the many that I owe; my total debt is $____ with monthly payments totaling $____. You can understand that my present net monthly income of $____ less drastically reduced living expenses of rent, food, utilities, etc., does not leave funds sufficient to pay even the minimum monthly payments to which I agreed.

Enclosed please find my check in the amount of $____, which represents the amount I will be able to pay each month on my account for the next six months. At that time my situation will be reviewed. I hope the payments will be increased regularly to allow for total repayment at the earliest possible date.

I respectfully request that the interest rate you are charging be reduced so that a greater portion of my payment will go toward principal reduction. Further, I request that during this recovery period, when you are accepting these lower payments, you not report this account as late to the credit bureaus as long as I make these new payments on time.

My financial recovery program projects that I will be completely debt-free within __ years.

I look forward to learning that you have processed this payment in acceptance of my request. If, however, you are unwilling to work with me as outlined above, kindly return the enclosed payment so that I can send an additional payment to another of my creditors who has agreed.

Thank you in advance for your cooperation.

Sincerely,

I hope that each check or money order enclosed with these letters to your creditors will be cashed. In my opinion, the fact that the payment was accepted indicates the creditor has agreed to your offer. You may continue to get phone calls, however, so receive them courteously.

Keep your recovery program and your commitment to full repayment uppermost in your mind. Whatever you do, don't miss a single payment and don't be late. After six months, contact your creditors again. Let them know how the plan is going, and tell them if you will be able to increase the payment.

Some people have had great success with this approach, while others have encountered creditors who don't want anything to do with renegotiating. But don't let one negative response defeat you. Send that creditor another letter in a week or two. Change the words, but don't change the message. Send it to the supervisor or the president of the company with an explanation that your offer has been turned down, but you are sure management will rethink this response. Be courteous but persistent, persistent, persistent.

Bankruptcy

Some financial situations are beyond repair. In these situations, there are few choices besides filing for bankruptcy. While bankruptcy can offer a fresh start for some, it can also turn out to be a 10-year mistake if filed in haste or without sufficient cause.

Do not think about filing for bankruptcy until you have considered and exhausted all other options. Once you have filed, it will be nearly impossible to get credit or rent a home or apartment. Many who have taken such a drastic step describe themselves as "financial lepers." Don't believe anyone who tries to convince you this step will be easy or a joyful way to start over.

It would always be advisable to contact Consumer Credit Counseling Services (800-338-2227) to find the office closest to your home before filing bankruptcy to get a second opinion. You may find you have a viable alternative through CCCS or some other qualified debt management organization.

If you decide to file, shop for a reasonably priced bankruptcy lawyer who will explain the pros and cons. I would be suspicious of anyone who tried to convince me it was all good and easy.

There are two forms of personal bankruptcy: the wage-earner plan and straight bankruptcy. Under the wage-earner plan, called Chapter 13, a court trustee supervises the full or partial repayment of your debts, usually over three to five years. Under a straight bankruptcy, or Chapter 7, the court apportions most of your assets among creditors. Federal law, unless overruled by stricter state limits, lets you keep up to a certain limit of home equity, household goods, auto equity, and other limited assets.

Many people who go through bankruptcy find a welcomed sense of relief, but the inevitable emotional toll should not be underrated. Bankruptcy will be on your record for life. Accept that. Even though it may drop off your credit report in 10 years, you will still have to answer truthfully whenever you purchase real estate or engage in other major transactions and are asked, "Have you ever filed for bankruptcy protection?"

If you must choose to declare bankruptcy, remember that nothing prevents you in the future from repaying the creditors you have harmed. If God so chooses to grant you the means in the future, I believe it would bring great honor to His name for you to go back and repay your debts.

No matter which way you choose to go, I hope that you will learn from your past experience and not go back to living beyond your means. Believe it or not, after filing for bankruptcy, you will become what some creditors consider a good risk. They will try to load you up with new debt because they know you can't file again for bankruptcy for a number of years.

Your fresh start should include living by the principles of this Money Makeover. They will help you get started on the right course and stay out of trouble.

During these difficult times, take care of your relationships. Don't underestimate the impact of bankruptcy on your spouse and children, both as part of the family and as individuals. You will all more than likely need to go through the stages of anger, guilt, and grief. In some ways, it will be like facing a death.

But don't lose hope. There is a new tomorrow, so pick yourself up, dust yourself off, and start all over again. Take courage from this letter-writer, who obviously stumbled badly but managed to regain her footing—and learn valuable lessons along the way.

There I was, a young single mother lacking direction, without child support, and battling depression. I took my daughter and moved to another city hoping to escape an abusive ex-husband.

I lived on credit as long as I could and ran up such a mess I figured my only solution was to file for bankruptcy. I saw this as a way to wipe the slate clean and treated the whole mess as part of the past. I figured I was entitled to a fresh start.

I found a way to get a whole new identity and a new set of credit cards and did I ever use them! I thrived on the instant gratification they offered. Eventually, I started my own business, which really sped up my debt-making abilities. I worshiped money and just couldn't get enough of it. It was my anesthetic of choice and deadened all the pain I was facing in my personal life. At one point I had 10 separate checking accounts.

I began buying real estate. At last I had found my niche, and no one was more surprised than I at my newfound business success. I learned to use every leveraging tactic known to the business world to mortgage myself into oblivion. I became a magician at juggling accounts, payments, and refinancing.

During the height of my career as a real estate tycoon, I married a wonderful man. He married an image, and believe me, I had created some image! Within a short period of time after we were married, I could no longer keep up the juggling act and my house of cards crashed. My new husband got to meet the real me.

We had no choice but to file for bankruptcy. I cannot describe the humiliation, the pain, the shame, and the disgrace of going through bankruptcy again—and this time dragging my new husband along with me. I hurt him, I hurt many other people, and I destroyed valued friendships.

The difference this time, however, is that we did not attempt to fix things by ourselves. I've taken full responsibility for what I've done, and I'm willing to learn from past mistakes. We no longer live to keep up an image. By turning our lives over to the control of God and applying sound financial principles to our lives, we have been able to pick up the broken pieces and put things back together. We have begun a formal savings plan, we pay our bills on time, and we've been able to buy a home. My priorities have completely changed as I am learning to discern what is important and what is not.

Filing for bankruptcy twice is something that I am ashamed of. However, in some odd way I am learning to be thankful for that, too, because as a result I am finally learning how to be financially responsible and content.

—Hydee

Chapter 12

It's Never Too Late

*Begin Turning Things
Around Today*

I received the following letter some time ago, and every time I read it,
I'm struck by the sense of desperation it conveys:

I've never written or told a living soul of our predicament as I am
embarrassed. At our age, most retirees are living comfortably on their
assets. But we are not. We are in our 70s and 80s and live on our
Social Security and a small pension. We live from one month to the
next, and it is a struggle. We always hoped to start saving someday.

159

We need to see if we can better ourselves, but I think it's too late.

Yes, we do have credit cards—six of them representing about $4,000 in debt. Our bills get paid on time, because even if we have to take it out of our grocery allowance, they get paid first.

Our debt may not seem large to some, but at our age it seems like millions. Neither of us can work anymore, so we feel trapped.

—Betty

The good news for this couple — and everyone — is that it's never too late to become what you want to be. No matter in which season of life you find yourself, it is not too late to get started with your own Money Makeover. It's never too late to start saving, to become filled with the spirit of generosity, or to make necessary adjustments to rein in your spending.

It's not too late to begin listening carefully to the quietest stirrings of your heart. It's not too late to start fulfilling your dreams.

Becoming who you want to be may entail a giant leap of faith. It may mean believing that you can hang up a shingle and make a living by following your dreams. It may mean casting yourself as the hero of your own story.

I allowed my eyes to get me into a lot of financial trouble. I saw nice things, and I wanted them. I wanted others to see me as prosperous and well-to-do. I didn't practice restraint, and I did everything I could to have things right now. The rest is history.

I was so busy amassing what I could see that I completely ignored the things I couldn't. My failure to see the invisible was my undoing. I didn't see the miracle of compounded interest—I didn't see what it was doing to me as my foe or what it could have done for me had I embraced it as a friend. I didn't see the underlying problems that drove my irresponsible spending habits. I failed to see the joy and happiness I was stealing from my future.

But it was not too late. I realized that unless I changed the direction I was going, I would surely end up where I was headed—in deeper and deeper trouble. I turned around. And you can, too.

As you begin the rest of your life with your new Money Makeover, look for the invisible. Embrace joy, choose happiness, and hold fast to the intangibles that cannot be taken from you.

Don't become a compulsive hoarder or a compulsive spender. Save, give, plan, anticipate, and then live life to its fullest!

And please, don't deny yourself the simple pleasures in life. Just make sure that if they have a price tag, you pay for them with cash!

> "Great peace have they who love your law, and nothing can
> make them stumble."
> —Psalm 119:165

Appendix A

The Best of
Cheapskate Monthly *Articles*

It's More Than Hunting for Bargains

Some people just don't get it. They have no idea what following the *Cheapskate* way of life really means.

Take the radio talk-show host in Charlotte, N.C., who recently introduced me as "the country's foremost bargain-hunter. Here she is, ladies and gentlemen . . . The Shopping Queen!"

Or how about the television producers who set up wacky demonstrations to show the world just how cheap I am—gags like separating rolls of two-ply toilet tissue to get twice the amount, collecting and straightening bent nails, and mailing utility payments without postage. Stupid tricks, for sure—entertaining perhaps—but a far cry from what I'm about and probably you, too, if you follow the *Cheapskate* philosophy.

The people I find to be most challenged when it comes to getting it are those who are momentarily speechless when they learn that I don't clip coupons, don't clothe my family at garage sales, and do not believe that buying things on sale is a great way to save money.

Got your attention, huh?

Let me remind you that bargain-hunting contributed greatly to landing me into more than $100,000 in unsecured debt. I taught myself how to see anything I really wanted as a bargain. That's all I needed to give myself the green light to purchase. *It's such a good deal, I'll take three!*

I'm trying to forget the time I made a hasty decision to purchase an above-the-ground, fancy-schmancy, 7,000-gallon swimming pool. Was it a bargain? Well, of course it was. It said right on the sign that the regular price was $3,900. And lucky me, I could pick up that little number for a mere $1,995. I told myself, *Just think how many needless trips to the river or beach could be avoided by having a fabulous water park right in our own back yard. And everyone knows there's no way to put a price tag on good family fun. Yep, it's a bargain.*

Brace yourself. *Cheapskate Monthly* is not subtitled *The Bargain-Hunter's Field Guide*. As a nation, it appears we have the bargain-shopping thing down cold. In less than 50 years, our cash-and-carry society turned into one that in the single month of August 1996 charged more than $3.3 billion on credit cards, 66 percent of which will become consumer debt.

So if the *Cheapskate* philosophy is not about finding great deals, what is it? Let me put it this way: If you were to place The *Credit-Card Junkies' Guide to Debt* at one end of the spectrum, you'd find *Cheapskate Monthly* at the far extreme.

The *Cheapskate* approach to life is about financial balance, which comes as a result of giving away part of your money, saving part of it, and then learning how to reduce the total outgo so that it ends up being less than your income. For the great majority of Americans, this is a concept so foreign that it nearly takes their breath away. And I'm as serious as a heart attack about it. Give first, save next, and then learn how to live within your means.

It's this principle of living within our means—reducing one's monthly expenses to fit within, say, 80 percent of one's income—that's the big challenge for all of us. It's not easy to go from living on 100 percent (or more!) of one's income to something much less. So we always look for new and reasonable ways to reduce expenses in every area of our lives. Finding bargains can certainly contribute to this quest to reduce expenses, but that represents only one piece in a much larger puzzle.

The *Cheapskate* philosophy is about getting out of debt—unsecured, killer debt. Nothing will sabotage your efforts to live within your means more quickly than spending your hard-earned income servicing consumer debt. While most debt-ridden consumers have given up on ever finding their way back to solvency, I'm here to tell you it's possible and I'm ready, willing and able to show you the way.

Another goal is finding financial peace, which means gaining the kind of security that comes when money for new tires and a brake job is put away long before the tires wear out or the brakes start to squeal. It's about being prepared for unpredictable, irregular, and unexpected expenses (previously characterized as emergencies).

Those who follow the *Cheapskate* approach acknowledge every person's unique income situation and personal preferences. Your means—the amount of money with which you have to work each month—may not be the same as mine, so your lifestyle may be far grander than mine. You may not be required to go to the extremes I must go in order to spend less than I make. And my means may allow for a lifestyle different from some-one else's. What's right for me may not be right for you, and vice versa. But as long as we are committed to no new debt and striving to live within our means by giving, saving, and spending less than we earn, we're getting it!

If you've become accustomed to spending more than you earn, can't get around to saving, and, quite frankly, have never even considered giving, the *Cheapskate* way of life may require a new way of thinking and acting.

Still scratching your head about why buying things on sale is not a great way to save money? When you buy things on sale, you might be spending less, but there's no way you're saving money.

There is a big difference.

Dare to Dream

I've got bad news about the American Dream. I'm pretty sure it's all but dead. I know. You didn't even know it was sick.

Ask anyone what the American Dream is and without fail the matter of home ownership will be in the answer somewhere. In a recent survey conducted by *Money* magazine, 82.3 percent of those surveyed listed owning a home as the number one most important element in their American Dream. With interest rates down and home values stabilizing in most areas, home ownership appears to be more available than ever. So how could the Dream possibly be anything but alive and well? Glad you asked.

Something seriously changed between 1929 when Bill and Agnes McAulay refused to buy a car until their mortgage was paid in full and 1994 when Chip and Buffy White bought their first home. Not only are the Whites stretching beyond reason simply to make their monthly payments on time, but they also hold absolutely no hope of living long enough to pay the darned thing off. What changed is our definition of home ownership.

To Bill and Agnes, owning their home meant *owning* their home. To Chip and Buffy, owning their home means *owning a mortgage* on their home. Owning a home used to mean having a paid-in-full note and an unclouded title—and hosting a mortgage-burning party. It meant making significant sacrifices until the larger goal was met. Now it means 360 payments, wondering if and when to refinance, unbelievable amounts of interest, and maybe second (and third?) mortgages. And just when the equity is starting to build a little and the payments become comfortable, home ownership invariably means trading into something bigger and better—picking up a new batch of even larger payments.

Come on! Paying off a home mortgage is something people did in the olden days. It simply doesn't happen anymore. I could count on one hand the number of people I know who truly own their homes—and still have three fingers left over.

With the price of a home averaging somewhere around 50 times what one cost in 1929, there is really no way anyone should ever expect to pay off his or her mortgage prior to their death, right? We've pretty much given up that dream as something only our grandparents could possibly achieve.

Well, hang on to your hats, folks, because I say let's take back the Dream! Sure, homes in the '90s are terribly expensive, but we really can't use housing costs as an excuse. That's because the average income has increased at a far greater rate than housing prices over the past 50 years. I believe that it is possible to pay off your mortgage early, own your home completely free and clear, and look forward to a truly carefree and debt-free retirement. Now is the time to get started.

1. *Formulate a plan.* Several good books are available to help you design a plan that works for your situation. Two especially helpful books are

A Banker's Secret by Marc Eisenson (Good Advice Press) and *Live Debt Free* by Ted Carroll (Adams, Inc.). What seems like an impossible stretch right now will become realistic in time, and your reward will be great.

2. *Stick to your plan.* Make the goal of owning your home your highest financial priority. Grab onto your plan like a bulldog and don't let go. Fix your eyes on the goal, and don't let anything deter you. Make a chart that clearly visualizes the difference between a prepayment plan and the original plan the lender set up.

3. *Teach your children.* Let them in on your plan. Teach the value of short-term sacrifice to accomplish long-term goals. Make home ownership something to be respected and sought after. If we intend to revive the American Dream, it's going to have to start in our homes.

4. *Plan a party.* Perhaps you've never even thought about it, but when that last payment is made, the lender really will send you the Note and Deed of Trust stamped PAID IN FULL. Frame the original—burn a photocopy in celebration of your great accomplishment.

For those of you who rent and feel that buying a home might be beyond your reach, here's my challenge: Stretch your imagination! Consider alternatives. There are programs available for first-time buyers. Get creative like the California gentleman who bought a house with a co-signer (because he couldn't qualify on his own). He promptly found two housemates to help him meet his monthly mortgage. Imagine how much more quickly he could prepay the mortgage if he found a third housemate and increased his monthly payment accordingly.

Start dreaming—and dream big! If you can dream it, chances are good that you can accomplish it. And don't forget to invite me to the mortgage-burning party.

Anatomy of a Supermarket

I never thought much about the logistics and intense marketing genius behind the supermarket business and all of the subliminal aspects until one day, in a tremendous hurry, I dashed into my favorite market only to find it had been completely rearranged the previous night. How dare they mess with my mind! The harder I searched for the items I needed, the more frustrated I became. In my usual timid manner, I went directly to the store manager to register my complaint and was told that this was just business as usual for a profit-conscious, modern-day supermarket. In frustration, I stormed out with only part of what I had intended to purchase.

Later on, when I had regained my composure, I went back and had an enlightening conversation with the manager. It seems that a store of that magnitude has pretty high overhead and allocates a large portion of its advertising budget to finding ways to appeal to customers' compulsive shopping habits.

It has been proven that the typical shopper quickly memorizes the layout of the store, knows exactly where to find the items needed, and becomes oblivious to products not regularly purchased. But by turning the place upside down every year or so, the store can "introduce" its regular shoppers to thousands of products they might never have noticed if the store remained unchanged. And to be ever so much more helpful, the merchandising experts determined that larger shopping carts would be nice. Ever notice how much larger those carts are than they were 10 years ago? They know that most people shop till the cart's full! I can only imagine what they are planning for the future. Maybe motorized carts complete with rearview mirror, turn signals, and optional trailer—all for the shopper's convenience, of course.

The average food shopper spends over an hour every week in a semi-comatose state shuffling up and down the aisles of the all-American supermarket, snatching item after item, building an expensive tower in a basket. At the end of the exercise, the score is tallied and in most cases the supermarket is the clear winner. The ordinary shopper is as predictable as a rat following a trail of cheese right into a trap.

The most expensive and frivolous items are usually placed at eye level. Baking staples such as flour and sugar are commonly on low shelves or so high up you have to reach for them. Eye-catching displays with lights, bells, and whistles usually promote junk-type and expensive items, even though they are piled up to appear to be on sale.

The center aisles usually house the prepared and brightly packaged, overprocessed food items. Either a hot-deli or bakery in the store will be emitting heavenly smells to appeal to your senses and start those compulsive buying juices flowing. The perimeter of the store is the safe zone— produce, dairy, and meat.

You probably can't avoid the supermarket completely, and it is difficult to remain completely true to your shopping list and financial plan in these kinds of stores. But you can commit to doing regular shopping in a no-frills warehouse store and enter the supermarket with extreme *caution,* fully aware of the many ways your compulsiveness is being tested.

It's a safe bet that food shopping will be more than an optional pastime for the rest of your life. You have two choices: either lapse into an even deeper comatose state or get smart.

Suffering Employment Insecurity?

It seems that the words *job* and *security* really do not go together anymore. All you need to do is pick up today's newspaper and read which company has just completed another major layoff (the term *downsizing* has become popular, perhaps because it sounds more reasonable than *massive firings*). Here is today's headline in my paper: "GM loses $4.5 billion, cuts to the bone; firm to close plants, slash 74,000 jobs; workers in shock."

I don't know about you, but I would much prefer a root canal without anesthesia to a blind-side unemployment hit!

These days unemployment has absolutely no respect. It is hunting down elite executives just the same as clerical and factory workers. Unemployment does not seem to be singling out any one particular part of the country, either. Forecasters of employment trends don't seem to be predicting any imminent change in the situation.

So what's the answer? Give in to the Three Ws—wish, whine, and worry? Hold a pity party? No, that wouldn't accomplish anything.

Try this analogy: I live in California, where the threat of earthquakes is pretty high. But I still live here voluntarily, and so do a lot of others. Areas of the East Coast live with the seasonal threat of hurricanes. But I don't see those areas becoming unpopulated any time soon. We have learned to prepare for these disasters. My kids learned "duck and cover" right along with fire drills from the first day of preschool. We have certain disaster plans in place—just in case. New California laws require every employer to have a safety manual in the event someone just happens to accidentally drink copier toner (among other potential emergencies)! My point is that we prepare for the most remote of potential disasters while leaving ourselves completely open to more likely crises.

Wise persons should prepare for unemployment. There are no guarantees for tomorrow. Rather than reacting to devastation with shock, a proactive posture seems far more appropriate.

Workplace Trends, a newsletter for management types, says that job security for both blue-collar and white-collar workers was a phenomenon that occurred after World War II and is now history. Today's corporate executive can plan to change employers on the average of seven times during his or her career—and not all voluntarily.

So I would like to unveil the Official Cheapskate Employment Disaster Preparedness Plan. Nothing new—just some focused common sense.

Part I. Do Everything Necessary to Stay Employed:
1. Consider your job a blessing. Obviously this is easier for some than others! If you "think thankfulness" for your employer, you might actually start feeling that way.
2. Step up your savings program. Experts say you need the equivalent of three to six months' expenses set aside for possible loss of employment. Impossible, you say? You can do it!
3. Become an expert on which alternative employment possibilities are available. Read the jobs available sections of the classifieds regularly to keep educated.
4. Start a file on employment alternatives. Learn what additional requirements you might need should you decide to make a career change.
5. Update your resumé—just in case. It's not a bad idea to review and update it every six months.

6. At the first sign of serious weakness in your industry or firm, step up your job search. Whatever you do, don't quit one job until you have landed another.
7. Make your decision to change jobs as unemotionally as possible. Trade in your nerves for excitement—two closely related emotions.
8. Weigh your decisions carefully. Don't avoid making a change just because you feel obligated to go down with a sinking ship.

Part II. In the Event of Unemployment:
1. Don't panic. Those who love and depend on you need you to stay calm and smart.
2. Don't pay off your debts with severance pay, stock plans, or any lump sums you might have received upon separation from your employer. You're going to need those resources for living essentials.
3. Determine how long you can hold out using your cash to cover the bare necessities. This will give you a clear picture of what you need to do.
4. Make a job-hunting plan. Network! You never know when Aunt Susie's hairdresser's husband's boss's sister-in-law's nephew might be looking for someone with your exact qualifications.
5. Keep a positive attitude, even if you have to fake it for a while.
6. Consider taking temporary employment provided it is in your field or profession.
7. Remember: Everything is going to be okay!

Sleepless in Southern California

In the middle of the night last Tuesday, I was lying awake thinking about mail. I get a lot of it. Mail doesn't usually cause insomnia for me, but this particular night it did. Not all of the mail, just one letter sincerely handwritten on yellow, lined paper and signed by a faithful reader.

Dear Mary,
I am writing in response to a letter you published in the November 1993 issue of *Cheapskate Monthly*. I am, in fact, very angry because the letter does not belong in your newsletter.

A woman wrote and said she decided to try your methods for saving money and paying off her credit cards. In three months, she has managed to save $2,500, and in four months, she will have paid off four of her seven credit cards.

Anyone who can save $200 a week does not have financial problems. Not only can she save over $800 a month, but she can even pay off four credit cards within four months. This woman is apparently rich. Please write stories about people who really have to change their lifestyles once they stop charging. It takes much sacrifice to try to pay for things with cash only, apply money to credit card bills, and also try to save a tiny bit, too! I felt I couldn't let this bother me any longer so I just had to write.

Sign me Discouraged.

I just couldn't sleep until I answered.

Dear Discouraged,

I believe you have missed the entire focus of this newsletter. It has nothing to do with "rich" or "poor." It's about learning to live within one's income, regardless what amount of money that might be. *Cheapskate Monthly* readers range from single parents struggling to survive at near-poverty levels to professionals making six figures per year . . . and more.

You might find it difficult to believe that within this newsletter's family there are members who make huge incomes, but because they have never learned to apply principles of financial responsibility to control their spending, they are in terrible situations. They pay huge amounts of interest, struggle to pay the bills, fork over staggering late fees, and dodge creditors. Their problems are no different from yours—just a lot bigger.

I'm afraid you believe the myth that all your financial problems would immediately cease if you just had more money, if you were "rich."

The truth is that unless one learns to live according to principles of financial responsibility—which include consistent saving, generous giving, and bringing expenses in line with income—more money will just make one's current problems greater. It won't solve them.

Unfortunately increasing one's income is the qualifier for more debt. That seems to have become the American way. Many people see an extra $500 a month as a way to get that new car or refurbish the house or handle a larger house payment.

Although most of us have great intentions of paying off bills with the additional income, the tax refund check, or the relief promised by a debt consolidation loan, unless old habits are replaced with new ones, the same debting patterns will return. Then eventually the original problem of not enough money will return on a much larger scale. The new and bigger problems will require even more money. Believe me, anyone can outspend their income. Greater income does not automatically insure financial responsibility.

I know nothing more about the California letter writer than what we both learned from her letter. Her excitement leads me to believe that saving and repaying debt is something new for her. Why else would she be so anxious to share her joy? Her new behaviors having to do with saving and repaying debt are nothing short of remarkable, as are yours.

The progress she is experiencing in handling her finances is what *Cheapskate Monthly* is all about! It is possible that the $200 a week she's been able to save is far below her eventual goal of saving 10 percent of everything she earns. Her struggles in that area are probably no different from your own. None of us knows just what changes and sacrifices she and her family have had to make in order to bring some sanity to their finances.

The purpose of *Cheapskate Monthly* is to help those who are struggling to live within their means find practical and realistic methods and solutions to their financial problems. If you don't think high-income individuals can have financial problems, you need to meet Donald Trump or Carl Karcher or any number of your fellow *Cheapskate Monthly* subscribers.

For the life of me I can't come up with one reason that would preclude that encouraging letter from appearing in this publication. I have a feeling she could probably teach all of us something about discipline and determination.

I hope that you will reconsider your reaction to the letter. To be able to rejoice in another's success could be a growing experience for you. When a member of our family experiences success I believe cartwheels are in order.

—Mary

Think Sacrifice, Not Deprivation

Every year, some national poll publishes the Top Ten New Year's Resolutions. Invariably number one goes something like this: "I'm going to get my finances in order." I'm not surprised, are you?

Considering Americans are deeper in debt than ever, bankruptcy filings are at an all-time high, and personal savings are embarrassingly low, I can only assume the obvious: Year after year the most popular resolution is dumped until the next New Year.

Budgets, diets, and New Year's resolutions must top the list of Things Most Likely to Fail. I think I know why. Each of them spell deprivation. Deprivation feels terrible, and we can handle it for only short periods of time before we simply cave in and give up.

I can't help but recall the times I attempted to stop using my credit cards. And I really tried to stop writing checks when there was no money to back them up. The problem was that cutting myself off from my ability to spend felt like a part of me was being ripped away—as if I was losing my security, comfort, and status in life. I felt like I was being punished and deprived of what I loved the same way a prisoner is deprived of freedom and personal choice.

Again and again I tried to reform, but the feelings of loss and the fear of deprivation were much stronger than any desire to change. A battle was raging inside of me, and I controlled neither side. Instead, I was controlled by overwhelming feelings and out-of-control desires.

The irony is that in doing so many crazy things to make sure I never felt deprived, I was paving the way for the ultimate deprivation—the total loss of everything in my life that truly mattered. I get chills recalling just how close we came to total financial disaster.

I've come to realize that the whole subject of reforming one's financial situation has two distinct aspects: Economics and emotions. If you have tried to cure your money ills only to fail, it's likely you were dealing only with the economics. Both sides demand equal attention.

I've found that dealing with the economic side of personal finances to be fairly simple, because it is so straightforward. It's math. It's adding and subtracting. It's agreeing that I cannot spend more money than I have and finding ways to spend less and keep more. When it comes to the economics of personal money management, there are right and wrong answers, black and white issues. And they're readily available in thousands of budget books on the shelves of libraries, bookstores, and homes of this country.

Then there's the emotional aspect of financial change, the part most ignored and least dealt with. Dealing with our emotions is much more difficult than handling the economics, because emotions are subjective. We see their result, but we don't understand them. We can't put them on a spreadsheet and move them around until they balance perfectly. We can't project them the way we project income and expenses.

I struggled because my emotions were so powerful that they overcame all economic good sense and rendered any potential change completely out of the question. That's until I discovered I can control my emotions. I cannot pretend they don't exist, but I don't have to be victimized by them, either.

Somewhere along the line in my journey to solvency, I made a profound, life-changing discovery. I learned that I could replace my fear of deprivation with the joy of sacrifice. I learned to harness my powerful emotions, turning them into my ally instead of my enemy. I purposely set out to embrace sacrifice and reject all feelings of deprivation.

Sacrifice means to give up something of value for the sake of something else that is more important or more worthy. Deprivation means to have a possession or enjoyment taken away. Sacrifice focuses on a goal. Deprivation focuses on poor me. Once I learned the startling difference between the two concepts, I understood why meaningful change kept eluding me.

The practice of sacrifice in the context of changing one's financial condition is a bit of an art form that is improved with practice. First, you must identify your more worthy goal. Without a purpose, your sacrifice will indeed be nothing more than deprivation. You need a worthy cause on which to focus.

Perhaps your worthy cause is to get out of debt once and for all, or take a once-in-a-lifetime family vacation. Maybe you want to allocate more money to give to your church. Or maybe your noble purpose is to save and invest money for your retirement.

Let's use the example that you're committed to be debt-free three years from now and to that end you are willing to make the necessary sacrifices. Just saying you're going to be debt-free is nice, but you need more than that. You need a written and measurable plan. You need a specific strategy that outlines exactly how you are going to reach your goal. You'll need to establish benchmarks so that you can measure your progress and look back to see how far you've come.

Focusing on the worthy cause and visualizing its importance and value is the way to combine the economic and emotional sides of financial change. Living each day with the goal in mind and practicing how you'll feel when that final debt is wiped out is the way to control your emotions.

I'm not suggesting that sacrifice won't be painful at times. The changes you will be required to make will be difficult. But when you focus on the more worthy goal, sacrifice becomes tolerable. With practice you will see the connection between a small sacrifice and the great reward.

If you've decided to make the journey to meaningful financial change, you're going to need lots of encouragement and understanding from your fellow travelers. We all need that because we are emotional beings—we thrive on approval and validation. We need empathy from those who understand what we're going through when the path gets steep and rocky.

As we make progress and reach our goals, we need encouragement to keep going so that we continue reaching for the next goal, and the next, and the next. Find people in your life who can offer that kind of support and reassurance.

These Friends of Mine

(The following article was in response to a letter I received from a frustrated subscriber, who wished to be known as "Bob.")

Once upon a time, on the outskirts of a village nestled in a beautiful kingdom, there lived a young man named Bob, his wife, Sue, and their young son, Bobby.

One day Bob, having just entered the fourth decade of life, gathered his little family around him and exclaimed excitedly, "We're right on target in building our future. We've paid off our debts (except for our mortgage), we have this lovely little cottage, we've saved and invested so well we now have $70,000 working hard for us. We have saved for Bobby's education and are well prepared to withstand the storms of life. We have a bright future. If we keep this up, we will be able to live in our dream palace by the time we reach the prime of our lives."

By and by, Bob and Sue became friends with others in their village. As their friendships grew, so did Bob's curiosity. Being lured to the bright lights of the other side of the village, he said to himself, *How in the world are these newfound friends of ours, who are of equally common heritage, able to afford such magnificent palaces complete with opulent furnishings, luxurious automobiles, and domestic staffs?*

"How can this be?" Bob asked them courageously. "It's no secret we all have about the same income. How is it that I can afford but a small cottage for my family while you live in such luxury? How can I, too, provide so well for my family and impress others in the village the way you have impressed me?"

"It is easy," said one of Bob's friends. "Do as we do. First you must give up your silly notions about saving for the future. You must agree to spend every dollar you earn plus every dollar you hope to earn in the future. Next go to the town square and gather about yourself plastic of every color. You will find a different piece of plastic in every shop. Soon new pieces of plastic will come to you automatically without request or inquiry. With all of your plastic, you must race out into the highways and byways and acquire everything you want."

Another friend chimed in, "Don't forget an Olympic-style pool like ours in which to exercise your lean, young bodies. In this way you will surely provide happiness for your family. We will even show you clever tricks like how to use your new plastic to make payments on your old plastic. Above all, you must eat, drink, and debt today, for tomorrow you may die!"

Terribly perplexed and feeling tempted to join his friends in their affluence so he could enjoy life to its fullest, Bob asked for an audience before the wisest old woman (meaning nothing more than that she was slightly older than he) in all the kingdom.

"Oh, Wise Old Woman," said Bob. "For all these years, I've done the right thing. I've saved as you taught me and my money has grown little by little through the miracle of compounding interest. I've carried a brown bag and gone without pocket money. I've planned all my spending. We've dined on sumptuous fare in the fine restaurants of the kingdom only when I could pay with cash. I've waited to purchase quality furniture for our small cottage until the proper amount of money was saved and the best deal found.

"My wife and young son do not complain," Bob continued. "It is I, Wise Old Woman, who see the palaces in the village. I salivate over the beautiful vehicles that make my paid-for cart look

sad. I am embarrassed. I want those beautiful things for my
family, and I want them now. What good is it to build for the
future when I may not live to see it? My friends say I should live
for today, for by the time I reach middle-age I may be dead and
gone. And then what good will all my planning have been?

"These friends of mine encourage me to gather about myself
plastic of every color and with it acquire a whopper of a palace
and all the furnishings and vehicles my heart could ever desire.
They promise me that only then will I find true happiness. If they
are right and these things truly hold the secret to happiness, I am
missing out by building for my future instead of living high on the
hog as they do.

"Please, Wise Old Woman. Is life really passing me by as my
friends insist? Am I doing the right thing or is it my friends who
are really right? Please reassure me before I haul off and do something stupid."

The Wise Old Woman, who had listened intently, responded
gently and knowingly, almost as if she'd been one of these friends
in another place, another time.

"Your friends mean well, my dear Bob, but they are nuts. They
are walking a high-wire while juggling very heavy debts. They
have no safety net. With arrogance they look to the future
demanding they be granted health and employment to someday
pay for all of the things they so foolishly feel they must have today.

"They are putting their marriages at risk with unthinkable pressure caused by the weight of the heavy debts. They are young
and strong right now, but in time they will become weak and
unable to keep up the juggling. They will crash unless they take
immediate steps to come down from the high life and learn to live
according to the wise principles you have learned. If they do not
change their ways, they will in time be surely bankrupt.

"What your friends say is true: Life is uncertain. Perhaps you
will be dead before you reach middle-age. But chances are far

180 THE COMPLETE CHEAPSKATE

greater, my son, that you will not die young and you will live to be 90 or even 100. Likewise your friends will live long lives and will face great sorrow as the foolishness of their youth destroys the joy of their old age.

"Do not envy them, young Bob. Instead pity them for the peril that lies ahead. Befriend them and be there to comfort them when the pain of crashing threatens to destroy them. Refrain from saying 'I told you so!' for indeed they will be in such misery, it will not be necessary. They will know.

"Continue living according to those wise financial principles that have brought you this far and have given you such a firm foundation. Do not allow your emotions to determine your attitudes. Your emotions cannot be trusted. They are fickle and change like the wind. Instead, work hard, give generously, save well, spend wisely."

With that the Wise Old Woman stood and reached out her hands to Bob and said, "You will now be highly revered in the land and shall from this day forward be known as the second wisest person in all the kingdom. Wear your banner proudly, for truly you are an example to which all the inhabitants of the kingdom aspire."

Feeling a sense of renewal and purpose, Bob ran home to the small cottage on the outskirts of the village nestled in the beautiful kingdom. As he burst into the small cottage, he gathered up his wife and young son and pledged to never again envy those walking the high-wire and juggling heavy debts.

"I've learned the truth this day," he exclaimed. "We will be patient to grow rich slowly and prepare well for our future. We will find contentment not in what we have but in who we are. I will provide for you, my little family. I will work hard, give generously, save well, and look forward to our bright future."

And so it was that Bob, Sue, and little Bobby from that day forward began to live happily ever after.

About a year after publishing this story in *Cheapskate Monthly,* I heard again from our friend "Bob." Much had transpired in that year, including the addition of a baby girl to his family:

Hey, Mary, it's me, Bob, the guy who lives "on the outskirts of the village nestled in a beautiful kingdom." I wrote to you last year because I was envious of my friends' luxurious lifestyles. But no more! The tables turned and now the friends who once made fun of me for being tight admit my style of life makes a lot of sense. Like many of your readers, my wife and I have worked our way out of all debt except for our mortgage. I must admit your suggestion that we also pay that debt off struck me as a nice thought but more likely a pipe dream.

Not long ago, our mortgage holder substituted detailed monthly mortgage statements for the old payment coupons. What a revelation! When I looked at the first statement, my mouth fell open. In the three years since refinancing our home, we paid only the closing costs and not one penny of principal. That simple examination started me thinking in new ways about our all-American, 30-year mortgage. A few quick calculations revealed that in 30 years we will end up paying for our house almost three times over! If we continue as we have, we'll pay $300,000 for our $100,000 home. But the real kicker is I will have to make more than $500,000 to come up with the $300,000, allowing for taxes and tithes.

Have we gone completely nuts?! Considering that most people move every five years or so and mortgages are set up so that little is paid toward the principal during those first years, millions of us are doomed to pay mostly interest for the rest of our lives. It's like throwing money in the trash. The average person will likely earn between $1 to $2 million in his or her working lifetime—and still end up broke. Between mortgage interest, auto financing interest, credit card interest, and taxes, over half of all the money the average person earns could go for nothing. I for one have had it with throwing my money away on interest.

Here we are, a couple who uses coupons religiously and closely watches every expense. I take a brown-bag lunch to work, we eat out one night a week, and we buy clothes during clearance sales. We wouldn't dream of going to a full-price movie, yet we're giving away hundreds of dollars every month to the mortgage company. Hundreds!

Our credit-crazy, monthly-payment, brainwashed society never talks about paying off a mortgage early. Such an undertaking is not only thought to be impossible, it's unthinkable! We live in a society that doesn't want us to pay off our bills. It wants us constantly borrowing and paying interest.

Like millions of our peers, we've been making our house payments each month and up until now assumed there was little we could do but ride it out to the bitter end. But the thought was just too depressing so I kept figuring and searching for a better way. We've decided to apply every available dollar to our mortgage, including the 10 percent we save. I've worked on this idea from every angle and the result is clear—if we stick to our plan, we will own our home free and clear in less than five years.

We will not sell our investments or touch our accumulated savings, but we'll stop funding them on a regular basis as we have been. We are now redirecting everything to prepaying the mortgage—the regular house payment, what we would be paying for a car, what we'd normally be putting into savings. In other words, all money not spent on living expenses and any extra funds that come along. Seeing that loan balance fall every month is the best feeling in the world. God willing, my wife and I will be 38 years old with no house payment five years from now.

When the house is paid in full, we'll resume investing 10 percent and put all the house payment funds into a Next-House Account. When we decide to move up, we can pay cash or assume a small mortgage that we'll pay down the same way. We definitely see a larger, more beautiful home in our future and feel this is the best way we can fulfill that dream.

—Bob

And my reply:

I think you have a fabulous plan! And I like your style—it's aggressive, no-nonsense, and determined. Interest is always a killer, but there's nothing like seeing the facts and figures of a 30-year mortgage on paper to get one's attention. You've discovered the secret the banking industry would just as soon you never find out: Advance payments stop the bank or mortgage holder from collecting compound interest on the amount you prepay—not just once, but month after month, year after year.

Since you have already accumulated savings and other investments, I think you are doing the wise thing by "investing" everything you can into your mortgage. That's exactly what you are doing when you apply your savings to that outstanding debt.

Mortgage prepayment represents a low-risk investment and the rate of return is guaranteed because making early principal payments will save you the interest payments you have agreed to make. It's a smart thing for someone in your situation to do.

However, I wouldn't recommend such an aggressive plan to the family carrying credit card debts or one with little or no savings. These folks need to first pay off those debts and work on accumulating savings equal to several months' expenses in case of a job loss or sudden illness. Nor would I recommend aggressive prepayment if one's home was showing a steady decline in value.

Well, my dear Bob, you've certainly lived up to your designation as the "second wisest person in all the kingdom," and I have a distinct feeling you've made the wise old woman very proud.

P.S. Maybe we shouldn't be too rough on the all-American, 30-year mortgage. After all, without that financing vehicle, few of us would ever be able to purchase a home. Such a mortgage might be the very thing that makes it possible for you to own your dream house completely free and clear someday soon! The key is to use the 30-year loan to acquire the property and then pay it back as quickly as possible.

Appendix B

....

Fifty Fabulous Ideas from Folks Like You

1. Do not pay for an unlisted phone number (also referred to as "nonpublished" in some areas). The fee for unlisted service costs anywhere from $1 to $3 a month. If for security and privacy reasons you choose not to let your name be published in the phone book and given out by directory operators, use your pet's name or the middle name of one of your children instead. Your security will not be compromised because if someone calls for your pet, you'll know immediately that it is probably not someone you care to speak with. —B.M., N.J.

2. Instead of throwing away a pair of pantyhose with a run in one leg, I wait for a second pair in the same shade to run, also in one leg. Then I simply cut off the "injured" legs just below the crotch. I wear both one-legged pantyhose at the same time with a newly created girdle formed by wearing both panty parts of the hose. I've saved big bucks doing this! —K.M., N.Y.

3. I never spend dimes. By adopting a personal attitude that the only thing I can do with dimes is save them, I consistently add $50 to $100 a year to my savings account—just in dimes! —R.D., Ill.

4. I discovered a great tip quite by accident. Every morning my husband poured the Efferdent water in which his false teeth had been soaking overnight in the toilet bowl. After a while I noticed that it cleaned the bowl so well that I no longer had to do heavy scrubbing with the weekly toilet cleaning. —M.B., Mich.

5. My mother colors her gray hair, but she buys Just For Men. It is half the

185

cost and lasts twice as long as what she was using previously. It beats buying the brands available for women, which are expensive and tend to give too much product for her short hair. —T.C., Ga.

6. Lint recently escaped my dryer filter and stuck to my pants instead. I grabbed the closest item I could find to try to brush away the lint. It happened to be a used Cling Free dryer sheet out of the wastebasket. I just ran it over the lint, and to my amazement all of the lint came right off. No more expensive lint remover rollers for me. —P.A.F., Calif.

7. Three scales worth their weight in gold: a 25-pound scale in the laundry room so wash loads are right—not too much and not too little; a five-pound scale in the kitchen to measure food portions for serving, freezing, and storing; and a 300-pound scale for weight control. The kitchen scale will also serve to weigh mail. No more wasting postage stamps trying to make sure you've used enough. You will know. —A.J., Ill.

8. Buy a three-pack of all-cotton white T-shirts to use as pajamas or beach cover-ups for small children. I buy a size large enough so the bottom edge is just below the knees. —J.D., Fla.

9. To keep milk fresh longer, add a pinch of salt when it is first opened. It doubles the useful shelf life. —E.G., Fla.

10. When I get the urge to purchase a new book, I call my library first. If it isn't in circulation, I request they order it. Nine times out of 10 the library will decide to add it to their shelves. Within a few weeks, it arrives and I enjoy the book for free. —L.N., Conn.

11. Most physicians are generously supplied with medication samples (also known as "stock bottles") by pharmaceutical companies. Always ask for a supply of these samples when your doctor prescribes medication. Doctors can even write a prescription for a stock bottle to be filled at the pharmacy for patients unable to afford the prescription. Asking for sufficient samples to make sure the medication is right is especially wise. There's nothing more frustrating than spending a

fortune on an expensive prescription only to find out you're allergic to it or it is not effective. Additionally, the Pharmaceutical Manufacturer's Association of America has a directory of programs for those who cannot afford prescription drugs. Call 1-800-PMA-INFO to determine if you might qualify. —S.Mc., Pa.

12. My favorite use for an empty 35 mm film canister is as a spaghetti measurer. Stack uncooked spaghetti into a canister. A full canister makes spaghetti for two—no waste, no guessing. I recently saw a spaghetti measurer in a kitchen shop with a $4.95 price tag. I chuckled knowing mine was free! —M.S., Wyo.

13. When I purchase meat that I intend to freeze, I always slip it into one of the free plastic bags from the produce department before I put it into a freezer-quality, zip-type bag. This way I can reuse the expensive zip-type bag again and again without having to wash it out or worry about bacteria contamination. No need to label the bag as I can see the label through the plastic. —M.H., Calif.

14. I use a no-tears baby shampoo to remove eye makeup. I learned this from an ophthalmologist I worked for. We encouraged our contact lens wearers to do this to reduce protein buildup on their lenses. Apply with a Q-Tip in a brushing motion while holding eyelid taut. — M.G., Texas

15. Here's a cheap, fun indoor activity for preschoolers. I pour coarse cornmeal (polenta) into roasting pans to make "sandboxes." The kids play happily for a long time with their little cars and people. The cleanup is pretty simple with a minivacuum. These kinds of pans are readily available at yard sales. I keep a large container of cornmeal (cheap!) on hand just for this purpose. —L.C., Calif.

16. Put cooking oil in a clean, plastic spray bottle. This is much cheaper than buying oil in a spray can and you can use the exact type of oil you want. —L.M., Pa.

17. I use Rit Dye a lot, especially when redecorating. I dyed my bedroom

curtains from peach to wine when we painted the room mauve. They turned out beautifully. Six years ago, I dyed my bathroom rugs from peach to green and now plan to change them to wine to match the new decor. (I never throw bathroom rugs in the dryer, since they have rubber backing. I believe this has prolonged their life.) Rit Dye can be found in all kinds of stores for under $2 a box. Follow directions carefully. —K.C., Ill.

18. I mix one part cornstarch to one part bath powder (my favorite is baby powder, but any kind will do), put the mixture in a pretty container, and add a nice fluffy powder puff. This extends the bath powder tremendously and feels great on the skin. People who are sensitive to fragrances could leave out the scented powder and just use cornstarch. It makes a good bath powder all by itself. I do the same thing with body lotions. I pick a favorite scent, buy a bottle of inexpensive, fragrance-free lotion, and add an equal amount of the scented lotion. Makes my favorite last twice as long. —M.H., Ill.

19. Orvus Horse Shampoo (available in pet stores) made my wool blend holiday sweater look better than new and eliminated the "scratchiness." My favorite elegant sweater with stones and silver threads was looking pretty tacky; it had really lost its luster. The dry cleaner refused to touch it. A lady who teaches quilting classes recommends this shampoo for laundering quilts and other fine things. It sounded crazy to me, but I figured I didn't have much more to lose. I was astonished at the results. Hint: Use only about one tablespoon horse shampoo to a sink full of water. —J.M., Wash.

20. I'm a major cookie-baker and enjoy lining my cookie sheets with parchment paper. I was paying $4.75 (or about $.20 for enough for one batch) a roll for the stuff at a kitchen specialty store. That was before I began living by *Cheapskate Monthly*! I asked around, and sure enough the local bakery counter will sell me parchment paper for just $.02 per extra large sheet (big enough for two of my cookie sheets). What a savings! —N.B., Kan.

21. When my automatic coffeemaker with a timer died recently, I was aghast at what a new one would cost. Here's my cheaper but better solution: I bought a less expensive model without a timer and an automatic timer device sold at a hardware store (normally used to turn lamps off and on automatically). I plugged my new coffeemaker into the timer. It works perfectly! —J.S., Mass.

22. Ashes from a wood-burning stove or fireplace make wonderful fertilizer for rosebushes. —K.E., Texas

23. Don't throw away all of your used laundry softener sheets. When you have an impossible-to-clean casserole dish or pot, toss one or two of the used sheets into the pan, fill with hot water, and *presto!* In 20 minutes, it wipes clean. No scrubbing needed. I store mine in an empty tissue box. —S.H., Fla.

24. Here's the jewelry cleaner professional stores use: Mix equal amounts of household ammonia and water. It's cheap, it works, and it's the best. —C.F., Wash.

25. I make an occasional trip to the newspaper in my area and buy newsprint roll-ends for about $1.50. There is always a lot of paper left on the rolls, and it is useful for wrapping gifts (can be self-decorated in limitless ways), stuffing packages to be mailed, and as "art" paper for murals, fingerpainting, and crayoning. I donate rolls to the local elementary school, where they're used for all kinds of projects. —H.H., Mass.

26. Use Murphy's Oil Soap (available in grocery stores in the cleaning product section) on your pet's dry, itchy, or flea-allergy skin. It is gentle and all-vegetable. Especially good for shar-peis with all of their skin problems. For an effective flea dip, boil orange and lemon peels in water. Cool and use for pet rinse or dip. Smells nice and fresh. You can also slice citrus and rub the fruit into the dog's fur. The bugs will keel over from the smell. —K.H., Calif.

27. Are your children's marking pens starting to dry out? Dip the tip of the

marker in water for about 10 seconds. Dry excess water, and you have just extended the life of the markers. —L.P., Ill.

28. The next time one of your leather belts wears out, don't throw it away. It will make a great collar for your pet. Just cut it down to size and punch a new hole. —J.F., N.Y.

29. Tired of throwing out celery that's lost its crisp and crunch? Cut bottom stem off and separate stalks. Fill a pan that is deep enough to cover celery with cold water and stir in 3/4 cup granulated sugar. Let celery soak for four or five hours. Drain well and refrigerate. —V.E., Colo.

30. Here's a recipe for inexpensive bubble bath: Mix 2 cups vegetable oil, 2 tablespoons shampoo, 10 drops perfume (optional). Beat at high speed for two or three minutes to emulsify. Keep in tightly closed bottle. Use about three tablespoons in each bath. —L.M., Pa.

31. Another good window cleaner: 1 cup rubbing alcohol, 1 cup household ammonia, 1 cup distilled water. Put in spray bottle and label. I like this better than the vinegar version. —C.R., Iowa

32. I give myself $100 a month allowance. I carry only $40 with me and put the remaining $60 in an envelope. Many times at the end of the month I still have most of the $60 left and use it to buy Texaco, Inc., stock, which can be purchased directly from Texaco with an initial purchase of $250 and subsequent purchases of only $50. There are no brokerage fees and all dividends are reinvested. Texaco, Inc., shareholder's services can be contacted at 800-283-9785. —L.C.R., Mich.

33. I enjoy going out for lunch on the days I work but usually forget to write down how much I spend and end up spending way too much. But I've discovered something that works great for me: On Monday I take $25 cash and put it in an envelope to be used only for my lunches. If it's gone before Friday, I have to take my lunch. This has really helped me to keep control of my finances without feeling deprived. —D.P., Fla.

34. Don't throw out that old silver chest designed to store silverware and prevent tarnishing. It makes a wonderful jewelry box. Earrings clip to the band designed to hold knives. Chains, rings, and brooches fit nicely in the open spaces, and nothing will tarnish because of the specially treated material that lines this type of chest. —A.B., Ill.

35. To prolong the life of swimsuits that are exposed to harsh chlorine, I purchase chlorine remover (either liquid or tablets) that is manufactured for removing chlorine from fish tanks. This product can be found in any pet supply store. I add a few drops of the liquid to a pail of cold water, pop the suits in when we're done swimming, and follow with a cold tap water rinse. —D.V.L., Wis.

36. To extend the useful life of dry staples—such as flour, meal, grits, pastas, and rice—pop in a couple of bay leaves. This won't affect the taste, but it prevents pesky bugs from ruining these products before they can be consumed. —C.G., Fla.

37. Here's great weed killer you can make for less than $2 a gallon. Dissolve 1 pound table salt in 1 gallon white vinegar (5 percent acidity is ideal). Add a few drops of liquid dishwashing detergent (helps plant material absorb the liquid). Label and keep out of reach of children. Use in an ordinary spray bottle. This nontoxic formula acts as a temporary soil sterilizer, so don't spray near roots of trees, shrubs, or plants you want to keep. I find it especially effective on my gravel driveway. I zap the weeds as they begin to appear. —V.W., Colo.

38. As a stay-at-home mom who loves to cook, here's how I earn money. I prepare dinner meals for two families in my neighborhood. Each family pays me from $8 to $10 per meal. The money I collect pays for all of the food for them and for my family. It's just as easy to cook for two as for 12. I deliver home-style dinners to the houses just before the families arrive home for the evening. This frees them up to spend time with their kids, I receive gratification from cooking, and my family eats for free. I use lots of coupons and always create the week's menus from

the weekly sale ads the stores place in my Thursday newspaper. —A.F., Calif.

39. If you are planning a wedding, contact a cake decorating class. You can coordinate with them to get a cake at an amazing price. I've done it. —M.C., Calif.

40. Here's how to make an effective, inexpensive heating pad. Take a clean sock (a man's tube sock with no holes works best). Fill halfway with about five cups of raw regular white rice. Tie a knot in the top. Warm in microwave on high at 30-second intervals until desired heat is reached. This heating device will stay in good shape as long as it does not get wet. I've been using the same one for more than a year. I learned this trick when I was in the hospital for a neck injury. This heating pad conforms well and is perfect for headaches, earaches, backaches, neck aches, cramps—anything that would call for a heating pad. —K.S., Ala.

41. We recently moved into an area where the water has a very high iron content. This discolored the inside of a brand-new dishwasher in less than six months and even the edges of some of my dishes. I tried bleach, baking soda, vinegar, Comet, and any other cleanser I could find. Finally, I complained to the builder. He recommended I try Tang Breakfast Drink! I ran an empty cycle and filled the soap dispensers with the powdered mix (it has to be Tang). The stains vanished. It is truly amazing. I have no idea why it works, but who cares? It does. —K.S., Wash.

42. When a good friend was expecting her fourth child, I hosted a rather unusual baby shower for her. Instead of the usual baby gifts, the invitations invited guests to bring a frozen dish, casserole, dessert, etc., for the guest of honor's freezer. They were also requested to bring a copy of the recipe. We presented her with a "cookbook" (using a photo album) along with a freezer full of food. It was fun and inexpensive and gave my friend precious time to spend with the new baby instead of in the kitchen. —J.S., Mass.

43. To remove residue buildup on your hair and make it shiny and bouncy, mix 1 tablespoon dry baking soda with the amount of shampoo you normally use for one hair washing. Repeat about once a month. This is a cheap substitute for expensive commercial products that do the same thing. —S.H., Wash.

44. Stop leaking ice-cream cones and their resultant disasters by placing a marshmallow in the bottom of the cone before loading on the ice cream. —L.F., N.Y.

45. Another use for dryer sheets: Use these sheets (new or used) as interfacing when appliquéing a quilt (the layer between the cutout and the quilt top). This keeps the quilt fresher longer between washings and airings, adds incredibly lightweight insulation, and extends the life of the quilt. —C.A., Mass.

46. To clean the inside of a glass thermos bottle, place an Efferdent denture cleaning tablet in it, fill with warm water, and allow it to sit overnight. —C.S., Ark.

47. I recently painted a bathroom and my kids' bedrooms for less than $20. I bought high-quality "mistinted" paint at a local home improvement center for just $3 a gallon and $.50 per quart. The colors are super and my kids loved it. Most hardware stores have bins of these kinds of "goofs" at near-giveaway prices. —S.G., Iowa

48. A kitchen accident left my white range top with an ugly chip in the porcelain. An estimate of $100 to repair the porcelain encouraged me to find some cheaper alternative. Liquid Paper (correction fluid from a stationery store) to the rescue! I gave it a try and to my amazement found it covered the spot and lasts a long time. I simply reapply every year or so. It looks great! —B.A., Neb.

49. If you have more time than money and need a new lawn, visit your local sod farm and purchase their "scraps," which are the odd-sized roll ends. You will have to patch it together, which takes time, but you can pick up these odd pieces at a tremendous savings. —D.D., Colo.

50. In discussing the price of medication with my doctor, we decided that if I bought the 100 mg tablet and broke it in two where it is scored, I could get my prescribed 50 mg dosage and the second month's medication for just a few dollars more. —S.I., Kan.

What Is *Cheapskate Monthly?*

Cheapskate Monthly is a 12-page newsletter published 12 times a year, dedicated to helping those who are struggling to live within their means find practical and realistic solutions to their financial problems. *Cheapskate Monthly* provides hope, encouragement, inspiration, and motivation to individuals who are committed to financially responsible and debt-free living and provides the highest-quality information and resources possible in a format exclusive of paid advertising. You will find *Cheapskate Monthly* filled with tips, humor, and great information to help you stretch those dollars till they scream!

Special Offer From *Cheapskate Monthly*

How to Subscribe to *Cheapskate Monthly*

Send check or money order for $18.00 to:

Cheapskate Monthly
P.O. Box 2135
Paramount, CA 90723-8135
(310) 630-8845 or (310) 630-6474

(Please call for Canadian and foreign rates)

Special Offer

Enclose this original coupon with your check
or money order, and your one-year subscription to
Cheapskate Monthly will be automatically extended
for an additional three months. That's 15 months for
the price of 12. Such a deal, considering $18.00
for 12 full issues is already CHEAP!!

(Subscription rate subject to change without notice.)

The Complete Cheapskate
Money-Back Guarantee

If *The Complete Cheapskate* doesn't show you how to save more money than the amount you paid for it, return your copy with your cash register receipt to the following address for a full refund:

The Cheapskate Monthly
P.O. Box 2135
Paramount, CA 90723-8135